SCAPA FERRY

A true-life story of courage and comradeship.

April 1st–5th. Two raids and three gales, in five days.

*The raids were confined to the main part of the
Flow and did not come our way. The battle-wagons
have come in from the western sea-lochs, and the
Luftwaffe seems to know all about it. Rumour has it
that a gentleman has been apprehended ashore after
sending a telegram through the Fleet Mail Office giving
details of all the big ships in the Flow. It seems
quite possible . . . .*

*The gales raged according to pattern. A raid warn-
ing went off in the middle of one of them, and the
barrage balloons were sent up. The one nearest us was
struck by lightning and subsided, porpoising madly, in
a plume of flame. Another dragged its attendant
winch-lorry into the sea.*

SCAPA FERRY

Antony Bridges

ARROW BOOKS

Arrow Books Limited
3 Fitzroy Square, London W I P 6JD

An imprint of the Hutchinson Publishing Group

London Melbourne Sydney Auckland
Wellington Johannesburg and agencies
throughout the world

First published by Peter Davies Ltd 1957
Arrow edition 1978
Reprinted 1980
© Antony Bridges 1957

Made and printed in Great Britain
by The Anchor Press Ltd
Tiptree, Essex

ISBN 0 09 916960 6

CONTENTS

INTRODUCTION

"Make paradise of London if you can,
You're welcome, nay, you're wise."
Bishop Blougram's Apology

MY STORY begins in London, those seven hundred square miles of bricks and mortar where eight million people are fated to exist.

London strikes different people in different ways. Perhaps I was unfortunate, in that two particular sets of opinions about it remained permanently beyond my understanding. One was that London was clean, when records proved that one hundred and seventy thousand tons of soot descended upon it annually. The other was that London was a desirable place to live in: a statement which seemed oddly at variance with the desperate efforts of millions of people to get out of it at every possible opportunity.

Perhaps a naval training is not the best preparation for a life in the Great Wen. Possibly, if I had been "entered" young enough to an office stool, I should have sat on it through the years with peace of mind and such peace of body as can be derived from golf and patent medicines. But I think it doubtful, for although a damaged leg had compelled me to exchange the Service for that prison life, I found many contemporaries who had been caught young, without any compulsion other than that of hopeful parents or a vague ambition, and shared my view.

Most of these friends were at the Bar, as I was myself. It was a profession which was still fashionable amongst young men who aspired to be barristers but had long since ceased to be so amongst litigants.

My real preoccupation—heretic though it might be, and

relevant no longer to the earning of my bread—was still the sea.

I joined several sailing clubs, and found owners of boats anxious for crews and always willing to stretch a point of patience and kindness to help a newcomer. Journeys to Norway and Brittany led to more ambitious excursions, so that eventually, of the three friends—two lawyers and a doctor—whose digs I shared, there was seldom a time when there was not one or more of us away in some boat or other.

The drawback to this amateur kind of sea-going was, of course, that it brought no pay.

Designers, and agents for the sale or delivery of yachts, could spend a good deal of their time at sea in the course of their business. But sailing small boats had nothing to do with the practice of the law.

When war came, these little prudential matters were put aside. Within a month my friends had disappeared into the services, and I was left to search for some loophole by which I could follow them.

Enquiries soon convinced me that such sailing experience as I possessed would not overcome the disqualification of a stiff leg for entry even into the Supplementary Reserve.

There remained the possibility of using some of the multitude of small yachts which would otherwise be laid up for the duration of the war. A suggestion for an inshore mine patrol was turned down, with a kindly letter, by a famous submarine officer who had been my Captain at Dartmouth.

A second thought was to use them for ferrying cargo.

A boat that is designed for one purpose can seldom be used for another. Many yachts, however, were themselves conversions from fishing boats, which had been designed for carrying considerable weights of fish. In any case, these small boats would be useful only for carrying small amounts of cargo, and work of this kind implied short journeys in sheltered water, for which everything that floated could be used at a pinch. It seemed that even sailing craft, provided they had auxiliary engines, might be suitable practically, if not economically, for this ferry work, so great would be the demand upon all larger craft for service work and for the longer sea passages.

Fired with this idea, and having the promise of at least one such vessel from friends who had gone into the services, I put the proposition in a letter to the Ministry of Shipping. I could not expect that an offer, emanating from a lawyer's bower in the Temple, of a small yacht for carrying stores would excite much enthusiasm in a government office. So, having posted the thing, I left London for a week, to make plans for a final throw, which was to convert a small sailing craft into an inshore trawler.

But the war, though it had not yet disturbed the smuts in the Temple, was bringing strange things to pass in the world outside. In the Ministry of Shipping (as it was then) a Captain Fisher was commandeering ships. And in a remote valley in Wales, a manufacturer, who had accepted an order for a potent cargo for a great naval base in the far north, was at his wits' end to know how to deliver it.

Turning into my Club at the end of that week, I found a reply two days old, bearing an official stamp.

Whilst I breathlessly digested the information that the Ministry of Shipping "appreciates your offer of several vessels of forty to fifty tons burden", the steward interrupted me to say that there had been a telephone message from the Ministry that morning. It asked me to ring up an exchange in North Wales with the improbable name of Penrhyndeudraeth. He was not quite clear what it was about, but it had, he thought, "something to do with explosives".

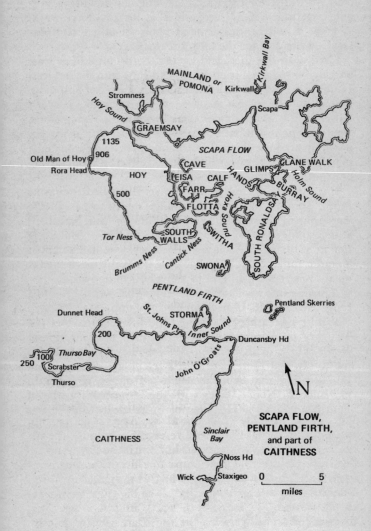

SCAPA FLOW,
PENTLAND FIRTH,
and part of
CAITHNESS

0   5
miles

1

SCAPA DESERTA

"Si vis pacem, para bellum!"
—Trite old truth

ON THE night of the 14th October, the battleship
Royal Oak, lying two miles south of Scapa Pier, was
struck by several torpedoes and sank in ten minutes.
In order to achieve this feat of arms, Lieutenant Prien,
in the U47, had entered Hamm Sound through a gap in
the line of blockships. It was discovered later that there
was not one gap, but two, and that he had entered the Flow
by one and left by the other.

On the 17th, German bombers, virtually unopposed,
raided the shipping at Lyness, and so damaged the old *Iron
Duke* that she had to be grounded in Long Hope, where
she became a store ship for the rest of the war. A Lewis-
gunner in an armed trawler so far forgot himself as to open
fire on the bombers without orders and bring one down.
It was the Germans' only casualty.

These disasters did something to wake up public
opinion, and would probably have caused the dismissal of
a minister who had been responsible for the naval defences.
Fortunately Mr Churchill was at the Admiralty, and he
could not conceivably be held responsible because it had
not been thought fit to appoint him until the day war was
declared. He gave out that Scapa would not be used as a
naval base; for obvious reasons he did not add "until its
defences have been put in order". The big ships were sent
to the western sea lochs, and, while attention was thus
diverted, the enemy agents in the islands were quietly

rounded up, and proper measures were planned and begun forthwith for working up Scapa Flow into a great permanent base.

Both physically and strategically, Scapa Flow is as fine a fleet anchorage as any in the world.

The main part of it is an enclosed sea, shaped roughly in the form of a rectangle eight miles by five, of an average depth of fifteen fathoms, quite unobstructed, and protected on all sides by islands. On the western side the island chain is doubled. The outermost of them, Hoy, presents to the fury of the Atlantic a long, unbroken wall, rising in places in cliffs over a thousand feet high. Amongst the inner line of low islands are bays and ramifications of the Flow, themselves large enough to shelter the entire Fleet.

To this great sanctuary there are—or were (for one is now a causeway)—five entrances, or "sounds": one in the north-west, Hoy Sound, one in the east, Hamm or Holm Sound, and three in the south, Cantick and Switha Sounds, divided by Switha Island, and east of these, Hoxa Sound, between the islands of Flotta and South Ronaldshay. Hoy Sound, the entrance to Stromness, is wide and deep, with a fierce ebb tide which meets the charge of incoming westerly gales in a fearful confusion of sea. The boom guarding this sound has to be placed further in, from the inner side of Hoy to the mainland of Pomona. Hamm Sound, in the east, is shallow, and during the 1914–18 war it was blocked by sunken ships—a barrage which had been inadequately maintained, as was emphasised by Lieutenant Prien. The three southern sounds can be blocked by mines or booms.

The islands afford complete shelter from the outer seas. Inside, there is sufficient drift across the Flow to prevent small craft running in the worst gales, but not enough to cause movement in an anchored vessel above the size of a destroyer.

The strategic importance of the Flow can be seen by a glance at the map. It commands the Pentland Firth. It lies

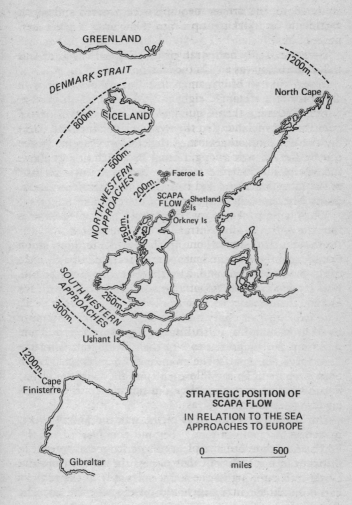

GREENLAND

DENMARK STRAIT

1200m.

ICELAND

North Cape

800m.

500m.

NORTH-WESTERN APPROACHES

200m.

Faeroe Is

250m.

SCAPA FLOW

Shetland Is

Orkney Is

SOUTH WESTERN APPROACHES

250m.

300m.

Ushant Is

1200m.

Cape Finisterre

Gibraltar

**STRATEGIC POSITION OF
SCAPA FLOW**

IN RELATION TO THE SEA
APPROACHES TO EUROPE

0   500

miles

almost equidistant from the approaches north and south
of Ireland and the passages into the North Sea between
Orkney and Iceland. To extend the circle, it is roughly
equidistant from the mouth of the English Channel and
the Denmark Strait. The whole north-western coast of
Europe, from Finisterre to North Cape, lies within two
days' steaming distance.

Its short-range strategic value, as a base for defence of
home-bound merchant convoys, was made absolutely vital
by there being so few facilities for discharging these
convoys in the west, and no canal by which vessels above
the size of drifters might pass from the Atlantic to east-
coast ports. Since the English Channel, after the fall of
France, became virtually closed to merchant shipping, all
convoys bound for the east coast were compelled to pass
into the North Sea by way of the Pentland Firth.

How much disaster, how much loss of life, how much
trouble and expense, and what grave peril to our existence
could have been prevented by timely action between the
wars no one can ever assess. The disasters are recorded; we
can count the loss of life; we can too easily forget the peril.
The expense—necessary and unnecessary—we know only
by its gross sum; but it is a burden which our sons and our
sons' sons will stagger under to their lives' end: till they
have forgotten what solvency means. Enemies have twice
been prepared. To say that each time they lost the war is
not to say that each time they did not nearly win it, with
far fewer resources.

During the first two years of the war the Moray Firth,
in range of enemy aircraft, became a graveyard. If the
Forth and Clyde Canal had been so enlarged as to enable
ships up to ten thousand tons to pass through it from the
Clyde into the North Sea; or, more cheaply, if the railway
had been extended to one or two of the western sea-lochs
and discharging facilities provided, the cost would surely
have been less than that of the ships and cargoes lost
between Cape Wrath and Leith, to say nothing of the men

lost, the time lost, and the diversion of fighting services needed to escort the convoys over the many hundred miles of extra distance.

At the same time, in spite of these omissions, it had not been considered necessary to maintain any military or naval establishments in Orkney.

It was largely owing to the enterprise of a private individual, Mr Cox, that the sunken German fleet, which seriously obstructed the Flow, had been removed by extraordinary feats of salvage.

The concrete emplacements for the shore batteries had been destroyed after the first war by Government order. Up to the end of 1938, there were in Orkney no booms, no anti-aircraft defences, no military or naval shore establishment, no oil storage, no fleet moorings, not even adequate roads. At Scapa landing there was nothing whatsoever but a pier suitable for small coasters. At Lyness there were about six hundred feet of deep-water quay, and a small wooden pier, which had been built in 1914 and was partly rotten. Naval headquarters was at Lyness, and for two years this pier was the sole landing place there for the personnel of the Fleet. Day and night, it was thronged with men and stores and beleaguered by launches and drifters, which lay alongside it five and six deep. In 1941, just as a new steel pier became ready for use, a drifter-skipper with a sense of humour hastened the wooden pier's demise by running into it at speed and knocking down the outer hundred feet of it; the drifter was unharmed.

After Munich, a few people realised that it was time something was done. Until the successive shocks of war, of Dunkirk, and of Mr Churchill's idea of leadership, nerved the country to consent to the necessary expenditure, much of the work could not be pushed beyond the stage of plans; but a beginning was made. At Lyness, the assembly of boom nets and moorings was begun, temporary oil stores were built, and buildings began to go up along the north shore of Ore Bay.

Most of the work, of course, was done by civilian contractors.

The contractor undertaking work in Orkney had to
tackle problems very different from those on the populous
mainland.

There was no accommodation. The site of the contract
was a bare moorland, usually separated from all sources of
supply by several miles of sea. There were no shops except
in Kirkwall and Stromness, and these were quite inadequate to provide for the extra population he would have
to import. He had first to estimate everything that would
be required, down to the last mug and blanket, for a camp
of possibly fifteen hundred men. Then he had to transport
it to the site, arrange for a regular supply of food, fuel, and
water, and build his camp, before he could begin work.

Transport was at once a paramount difficulty.

The sources of supply were all in the south. The normal
shipping point was Leith. But the Luftwaffe's sweeps over
the two great Firths which drive wedges into the eastern
side of Scotland focused attention upon an alternative
route.

North of Invergordon there is only one harbour fit to
handle traffic. This is Scrabster, a tiny place, tucked into
the corner of Thurso Bay, twenty miles west of John o'
Groats. There is a single-track railway from Inverness to
Thurso. A two-mile extension of this line to the harbour
at Scrabster had been proposed during the first war but
never carried out. The cargo had therefore to be carried
by lorry from Thurso to Scrabster. The crane at Thurso
would lift five tons; that at Scrabster fifteen hundredweight. Cargo, if sent by the Scrabster route, had therefore
to be (1) limited to individual lifts of five tons, or such less
amount as could be handled from the lorry by the derricks
of the ship into which it was to be loaded at Scrabster, and
(2) strictly limited in amount, to avoid congestion on the
attenuated railway. The only alternative was to ship it

from further south and run the gauntlet of the enemy bombers.

A further difficulty the contractors had to face, as soon as war broke out, was shortage of ships. While peace lasted, it was relatively easy to find space for a moderate amount of cargo in the regular Orkney steamers sailing from Leith and Scrabster. For a bulk cargo it was possible to charter one of the many coasters plying for hire. By Christmas, 1939, one-fifth of all merchant tonnage had been absorbed by the services. Their demands fell with special weight upon vessels operating on the east coast of Scotland, for Rosyth and Scapa were in that neighbourhood, and the authorities there grabbed what they could reach.

When it came to explosives, the chances of transport almost disappeared. Nobody liked it, even in time of peace. It required special fittings; it affected insurance; and it would not mix with passengers and mail. With enemy bombers keenly on the watch, it became rank poison. Shipmasters might be indifferent to the added risk, but they were by no means indifferent to the extreme complications it caused.

I knew nothing of all this, as I sat in my chambers in London one day in that autumn of 1939, talking to a Mr Harrison, who had come to see me about a job of work. Sixty tons of blasting gelignite, to be made by his firm, were needed in Orkney for a big Admiralty contract, and he was seriously suggesting that I, an unknown amateur yachtsman, might carry it across the Pentland Firth in a small auxiliary sailing cutter.

The day happened to be the 14th October—the day the *Royal Oak* was sunk.

2

A CONTRACT & SOME OF
ITS IMPLICATIONS

"Not in the beginning of enterprises,
but in the thoroughly performing and finishing the
same, lyeth the chief glory."

I LISTENED with mounting excitement while Mr Harrison quietly explained what he wanted me to do.

"We have," he said, "what is called a 'blanket' order for twelve tons of gelignite. As you probably know, this means that the delivery of each lot is not specified beforehand but is made as required. Only twelve tons is certain. As far as we know at present, delivery will be required at Lyness in five-ton lots at intervals of about a fortnight. The proposal at present is to consign by rail to Thurso, and to ship from Scrabster to Lyness. What do you think of that?"

What did I think of it!

An eight-hundred-mile sail to the north of Scotland in the middle of winter. In war-time, with the chance of being gunned by our own people without warning if we happened to be near the coast at night, though attentions from the enemy at this stage could probably be discounted. Then the Pentland Firth, where the tide runs at ten knots and the seas had swept a cruiser clean of superstructure in the last war. Five tons of dynamite thrown in. I had been thinking in terms of potatoes from the Isle of Wight!

"Let us have a look at the map!"

I found an atlas, and opened it out amongst the red-taped bundles on the table. We bent over it together, and I did some pretty hard thinking.

The journey north might not be so bad. We should have to go westabout. That way, we should avoid enemy aircraft, and have sheltered water from Kingstown to Invergordon, via the Crinan and Caledonian Canals. I had been up to Skye during the summer, and knew the road as far as Lochaber. The only two badly exposed bits were, first, the mouth of the Bristol Channel, and, second, the long slope of the Moray Firth to Wick. There, we should just have to watch the weather.

Now for the Firth itself. I had never seen it, and knew it only by its sinister reputation. I remembered a phrase or two from the Pilot Book. "All distinction between air and water is lost." And, on the other hand, a prim encouragement: "To pass the Firth is not beyond the capacity of a competent navigator." I always felt that the author of this book tended to be a little lyrical in some of his standard expressions, such as "cast to instant destruction"; yet, of course, it could happen.

Claud Worth had a note somewhere on the Firth. What was it? I remembered reading it, in the fascinated way one is apt to read about horrors; and remembered, too, that, in his quiet way, he gave, as he always did, the key to the problem: "In bad weather these waters should be avoided at all costs, *and I should not care to turn through the Firth with a spring tide against even a fresh breeze*. But under favourable conditions and with proper management there is nothing to fear, even in the smallest yacht." Wind against tide—that was it. Avoid that conjunction, and "there is nothing to fear".

How wide was the Firth? Ten or twelve miles. Say twenty miles on the slant from Scrabster to Switha Island. Say four hours. And only one return journey every fortnight. Surely there would be two four-hour spells in fourteen days when it would be possible to cross, even in a little boat.

"Well," said Harrison, looking keenly into my face, "what do you think?"

There was never any doubt in my mind that I was going to try this thing.

"I think it might go," I said. "But there's only one thing I can promise you: that I'll do my best. How much time can you give me?"

"The first load is expected by the end of December. You haven't said anything about payment yet, Mr Bridges."

We looked at each other, and laughed, and I began to like Mr Harrison very much indeed.

"For work of this sort," he went on, gravely, "we can offer fifteen pounds a ton, from Scrabster to Lyness. As I said, twelve tons is all we can be certain of, at present. The total requirements are at least sixty tons. If we get the whole of that order, we shall hope you will carry it for us, and in that case we shall ask you to accept a reduction in freight to about ten pounds a ton. Whether we shall get it or not, I don't know. That may depend to some extent on you!"

Twelve times fifteen, I thought, how much is that? I found a pencil and wrote it down. A hundred and eighty pounds! It seemed an enormous sum.

Harrison was getting up to go. "I shall have to report to my firm," he said. "We will write or telephone within the next two days."

"All right. Let us leave it, then, that I will put as much as possible in train—crew, permissions, and so on, and, as soon as you give the word, we'll start fitting out."

Fitting out! I had not only to fit out. I had to provision a fifteen-ton boat, for a crew of at least three, and take her eight hundred miles. How it was to be paid for I had no idea. I only knew that it was going to be done.

Bursledon. A little boat, lying on the mud in a rank of assorted craft. The mast still in her. She is about forty feet long on deck, eleven feet beam. Straight bow, curved forefoot, and wide, dished counter—too flat, but never mind. Bulwarks, coach roof, and wide side-decks. She is a King's

Lynn pilot cutter of fifteen tons, built in 1908, and her last survey, made a year ago, says she is sound. Name: *Mermaid.* "The chief ship, whereupon I trusted, called the Mermayd of Dartmouth. . . ." I'll pass that!

Straight wood keel, handy for taking the ground. All inside ballast—four tons of iron bars on a concrete footing. There is nothing much inside—no fancy work, thank goodness; only matchboard partitions. Two quarter-berths; cabin, about nine feet long; and fo'c'sle. A 14-h.p. petrol engine in the quarter-berth space on the starboard side.

Measure the cabin carefully. In it will have to go two hundred boxes, each twenty-five inches long, nine and a quarter inches wide, seven and a quarter inches deep. They will fill the bunks, the cupboards, and rise five feet from the floor. What will they do to the centre of gravity? Goodness knows. They will certainly bring it up. We will take out only a little ballast, and take half a load, the first time.

The mast is rotten at the hounds. The standing rigging doesn't look too good, either. I must have handgrips made and fitted to the cabin top.

Telegram to various boatyards:

"Please quote cost and earliest completion for solid pole mast forty-seven feet overall eight inches diameter at deck very urgent."

(By telephone):

"Look, darling, don't bet on this. I think Harrison took a good view, and obviously they are very badly stuck for transport. But his bosses may think differently. Myself, I think it's fantastic that they should even consider . . .

"What? No, of course I pushed it to the limit. Turned on everything I had—aspect enthusiastic, but subdued!

"Now, how soon could you get clear of your Fire Service? If he says Yes, we shall have to move fast.

"All right. Do what you can. Tell them it's top secret and vital to the safety of the nation! They *must* let you go.

Hang it all, you've done twenty thousand miles in small boats. Surely that's more than you've done in a taxi!

"Yes, my dear, sooner you in a thing like this than anyone I know—*anyone!* They ought to have given you an M.G.B. by now, if you'd had your rights. After all, what are we going to be married for? Sorry—you know what I mean!

"I'll try Kirk—he might come. There simply isn't anyone else. They've all gone. But we'll be in Scotland before them—we say so, and we hope so!"

"It's crazy, Tony!"

"I know it sounds steep, Kirk, but I think there's a reasonable chance."

Another tense silence, while we sip the good port that Kirk's club provides. I have put all I have got into the last half-hour. Amid these deep chairs and marble columns, this atmosphere of gravity and comfort, it does sound rather crazy. But J. B. Kirkpatrick knows about the sea. He has lived on it, and he has written books about it. He loves it. And he knows about the cold and the wet and the weariness of it. He is older than Margaret and me—a good deal older —old enough not to be quite so keen, quite so careless of himself. Too old to be accepted for a Service, like most of our other friends have been. Yet, that must rankle, too.

Am I right to ask him to come? It may be hell—it probably will be. Yet he knows boats. He can cook marvellously under any conditions. He would help us through. In fact, he is my only hope. And we *must* have someone we can trust. There will be only room for three, and none of them can be a passenger.

For a long time Kirk's dark, sensitive face looked past me without expression, as he thought it out—thought me out—twisting the stem of his glass slowly between his long fingers.

"It's crazy," he mused again, half to himself.

I had no more words.

"But I'll come," he said, and looked suddenly at me with a quick little smile, that made him seem ten years younger.

"Don't touch it!" said my friend, the yacht agent, savagely. "For God's sake, don't touch it!" He replaced his sextant carefully in its mounting, and snapped the box shut, for he had been taking a navigation class and wishing he was back at sea.

"Oh, yes, you'll get there, and you'll manage well enough for a time." (This, I thought jubilantly, from an extra-master!) "But, sooner or later—mark my words—sooner or later, you'll have a smash! And then your expenses'll start!"

"I wouldn't advise it," said the Founder gently.

I sat on the edge of my chair in the Club, looking reverently at this man, to whom I had put my case. He probably knew more about sail than any man living.

"I've been passed fit for sea, at sixty!" he went on, with a smile.

"What are you going to do, Sir?" I asked.

"Ocean-going tugs, I think. Salvage. There'll be plenty of that, when the U-boats really begin."

"I'd say yes to your plan if it were anywhere else," he went on. "But the Pentland Firth! In winter!" He shook his head. "It's a bad place. However, I don't suppose you'll let me stop you! If I can do anything to help you, let me know. Good luck!"

Two telegrams, written down by the clerk at my chambers, and handed to me with a look of offended dignity:

From Morgan Giles, Teignmouth:

"Price for mast fourteen pounds delivery ten days."

From Cooke's Explosives, Penrhyndeudraeth:

"Agreed. Proceed in terms conversation 14th. Will confirm. When can you start?"

So, it was on! I stood for a moment, looking out at the tiled wall of the area, with its drab mysteries of pipes and gutters.

> "Heaven hath her high as Earth her baser wars.
>   Heir to these tumults, this affright, that fray,
>   Peer up, draw out thy horoscope and say
> Which planet mends thy threadbare fate or mars!"

Anyway—to work!

3

UNDER WAY

"We gnaw the nail of hurry. Master, away!"
Hassan

5TH DECEMBER, midnight. At sea off Berry Head. A
bright moon casts its radiance over sea and cliff, and
the *Mermaid* is crashing along in calm water with a
strong offshore breeze. It is as cold as charity. Inland, it
must be freezing hard tonight. But it is good to be here,
chocked off again in the cockpit of a little boat, well rugged
up in sweaters and oilskins, surrounded by this glory of
moonlight. It is good to feel the tiller under my arm again,
and to listen to the whistle of the wind, as it presses out of
the taut curves of the sails, and to the crash and hiss of the
sea about the boat's hull. Good to be clear of the land!

We are taking a chance in sailing so close to the coast
at night. We are not supposed to be within three miles of
it. But we are late on our schedule, and must seize every
chance the weather offers. As far as I know, there aren't
any guns on Berry Head. We will go well clear of Start
Point, and if this breeze holds we should be at the Lizard
tomorrow night. From there, even if it goes back into the
west, we shall be free and clear of everything up to Milford.
We are under way at last—and about time, too!

I would not willingly go through the last six weeks again.

At times it seemed as if we should never get away. At
first, Harrison's firm changed their minds and thought the
whole thing too uncertain. Then they wanted us to load
at Portmadoc. I did have the sense to turn that one down.
The vision of a night passage in dirty weather, the watch

below trying to sleep with its nose against the skylight upon
a plunging four-foot stack of gelignite, while Kirk balanced
his pots upon a naked Primus, was too much even for my
enthusiasm. Captain Fisher, at the Ministry, clinched the
matter by saying that under no circumstances would we be
allowed, loaded, through the Crinan and Caledonian
Canals. So Scrabster it had to be.

Our chief difficulty is that we have no official standing
whatsoever.

What we are, I suppose, is a partnership of independent
private contractors, and the *Mermaid* therefore ought to
be a merchant vessel. Captain Fisher wrote on our behalf
to the Mercantile Marine office at Southampton, and we
got as far as a survey and a letter giving provisional
measurements. But there was no time to complete the
registration. To do that, one has to produce documents
tracing the ownership back for the previous fifteen years.
I was not even sure whether a boat of less than fifteen tons
was capable of registration as a merchant ship. But we had
to pretend to be one, in order to satisfy the Board of Trade,
and we had to pretend to be, at any rate, something other
than a yacht, in order to satisfy the Naval Control, since
all movements of yachts have been stopped.

I doubt if we should have got away from the Solent at
all if it had not been for an extraordinary piece of luck.

I had taken the bus into Portsmouth to report to Naval
Control, and arrived outside the office just as the staff were
coming out to lunch. As I watched them, with the awe of
an ex-cadet at being in such proximity to so much gold
braid, a lean figure in Vice-Admiral's uniform came out of
the door, and I realised with a shock that he was a cousin
of mine.

He asked me to dinner that evening, and I told him my
yarn and then waited to see if I was to be smacked and sent
home. I was none too hopeful, for I had no illusions that he
would provide me with a destroyer escort out of the Solent.

He did, perhaps, more than he should have done. Next

morning, I was given an order for ten gallons of petrol, a promise that the forts at Hurst Castle would be told to let us out, and a Naval Message form stamped with the office stamp and bearing the pencilled instruction "Please assist Bearer if at all possible". It was delightfully non-committal. But it worked!

Margaret and I sailed next morning for Teignmouth, where the new mast was to be fitted (and where Kirk was to join us).

At Hurst Point, we were held up for more than an hour by an examination launch. By that time, the sun was setting and there was only half an hour left of the fair tide. The wind had drawn round to the west. We began to tack across the channel, making less and less ground at every leg as the flood strengthened. It got quite dark. Searchlights stabbed out from near the water on the Isle of Wight shore and fixed us curiously in their white glare. The wind freshened and it began to rain.

We held on, determined to struggle clear. Going below to light the cabin lamp and cook some food, Margaret reported that the glass was dropping fast. When we had come abreast of the Needles, steaming lights appeared astern and a searchlight snapped on. It was our friend, the examination launch. He shouted to us to come back and anchor under Hurst Point.

It blew hard that night and all the next day.

On the morning it cleared, we were up early, and were surprised in the middle of breakfast by a lieutenant-commander, who boarded us from the big examination yacht at Yarmouth. We had not made up our beds. Plates and mugs were all over the floor, for we had no table. And I hadn't shaved. There were a lot of questions, directed mainly at Margaret, which we answered shortly enough, for I was very cross at being taken at this disadvantage without even a hail.

Matters were made worse when we at last got under way,

for we lost our dinghy in the wash of tide and had to have it retrieved for us.

The passage to Teignmouth was uneventful, except for a hint of war in the night, far south of Portland, where the thud of gunfire came from somewhere below the horizon, and the yellow globes of star shells hung for a long time in the vault of the night, outshining the moon.

At Teignmouth, Mr Morgan Giles himself met us with a dinghy and took us ashore to see the new mast, brought up specially from Plymouth in the form of a great baulk of Oregon pine, twelve inches square. It was already rounded on the trestles to nearly its finished size. I waited only to see the *Mermaid* warped under the crane for removal of the old mast, and then, leaving Margaret to superintend the refit, I went to London to settle our few affairs and tell Kirk we had made a beginning.

While I was there, telegrams came from Teignmouth in disturbing succession. "Mast broke at the hounds whilst lifting out." "Wire rigging all rotten. Must renew." "Suggest new halliards and new mainsheet. When are you coming?"

Kirk and I arrived three days later, to find Margaret and two others working at top speed at the vices in the riggers' loft, surrounded by a mass of wire and manilla. Most of the old gear was quite rotten. The enforced delay in the Solent on the night the gale broke had been providential.

The *Mermaid* lay a week in Teignmouth, whilst her crew worked and journeyed incessantly with boatloads of gear and stores. The weather was fine whilst we worked, but on the morning of the 3rd December, when we were ready to sail, the glass was dropping and the wind was in the old cyclone quarter, south-west. However, our time was running desperately short and we determined to start, for west of Teignmouth there were many harbours we could slip into if it got bad.

Like most of us, I suppose, I have a Little Man, who comes and makes unnecessary remarks to me when I am feeling more than usually stressed. At three that afternoon, with the western sky all flat and hard, the seas grey and pitted like cast steel, and the *Mermaid* reefed right down and making no headway at all, he hung somewhere in the lee rigging, over the foaming side-deck, and began a peculiarly tiresome inquisition.

"Do you really know what you are doing?" he whispered in a freezing tone, that was more chilling than the gale. "Do you really think you are going to get to Scapa Flow? You see, she won't even go to windward—not in a hard blow! What happens in a real gale? Suppose you get jammed on a lee shore! You'd never beat her off!"

After waiting awhile to let that one sink in, and to chuckle as a solid top smashed over my head and by-passed the towel round my neck, he went on:

"You've never been to sea in winter before, have you? Air is cold and heavy in winter, isn't it? Knocks a sea up in no time. Seven hundred miles north it will be colder still. Suppose the decks got iced. Another ton or so of top weight added to your five tons of gelignite! Gelignite—ha! And as for seas, remember, this is only the Channel. What about the Pentland Firth, with this wind against an eight-knot tide? Scapa Flow—ha, ha! Will you ever be holding that tiller, as you are now, in Scapa Flow?"

I told him I didn't know—quite possibly not; but that there was a war on. Meanwhile, since there was no hope of making Dartmouth, I was going in to Brixham. He laughed again, in a wounding sort of way, but had to take himself off, as he always does when I am busy.

Shouting to the others to slack away the main sheet, I pulled the helm up. The bow fell away until it was pointing towards the cliffs and the boat at once gathered speed. Then, with the main sheet slacked out, the end of the long boom tripped into the sea on the leeward roll. As the ship lifted on the next crest, it swung out with a crash.

I put both feet against the far side of the cockpit and hauled the tiller hard up. The bow fell off a little more, and then, as the boom dipped again and forced the main-sail aft against the wind, it came up obstinately to the broadside course.

The cliffs were about a mile and a half away, but at the rate we were going we should hit them in a little over ten minutes. At this point we realised that we could not lift the boom up, clear of the sea, because there was only a single topping-lift and on this tack it led the wrong side of the sail. The situation was becoming ludicrous.

Rather than wear round we at last got her to pay off, and she raced away hectically, kicked, hurtling, up the slope of each following sea, and settling, with a roar of bursting water, as the crest passed underneath. At every roll that infernal boom tried to dip itself into the sea, and then, as it lifted clear, to crash forward again with the weight of wind, till I feared for the blocks and for the boom itself. The wind was right aft, and a gybe would have taken the mast out of her.

However, there was not far to go, and soon we were in a blessed peace of calm water, sheltered by the two-hundred-foot cliffs of Berry Head. In a downpour of rain we anchored inside Brixham breakwater and stowed the sodden sails. Then we stripped to the skin and put on dry clothes, and felt suddenly tired and hungry.

For the next two days the gale raged, veering through north to north-east, after the standard pattern, and blowing itself out in an arctic fury of sleet, which gave place gradually to gleams of cold sun out of a ragged blue sky.

During that time I had another session with my Little Man. He took the line that the *Mermaid* was now proved, by demonstration, to be inadequate to the job; that it was only vanity which had started me on this crazy enterprise and only vanity that would make me go on; that, if I did go on, I should have the lives of two other people on my head, as well as my own. All the time he reminded me mad-deningly of the delay, and suggested that, as things stood, it would be perfectly reasonable and honourable to call the whole thing off, and use the *Mermaid* to go fishing instead! Had I been alone, he might perhaps have won his case at this point. But he made the mistake of putting his arguments in Margaret's presence. I saw her simply turn her dear face in his direction and go on talking to me as though he had never existed, and he couldn't stand that.

By the evening of the 5th the gale had dwindled to a steady offshore breeze, and the glass was still rising.

We went up to the yacht club to hear the ten o'clock forecast. It was good—good enough for us to sail.

We took our drinks to the window of the warm, well-lit room, and looked out over the harbour, where the path of the moon was ruffled by the cold night wind. Kirk was talking to some of the members behind us at the bar. Margaret said to me: "Well, what do you think of it?"

I looked at her, so keen and so happy, and for a moment my heart sank and the dim outline of the Little Man flickered beyond the window pane. But he had had his say.

"I think it looks all right. But I wish I was in my little downy bed!"

"Don't let's waste it, then. Come on! An offshore wind and quiet water to the Lizard—I believe we are going to get a break at last!"

4

TROUBLE AT MILFORD

"I wish to heaven we had never come in
here; it comes of landing, *ever!*
The Riddle of the Sands

THERE IS a blank in *Mermaid*'s log between the 8th
and the 17th December. The events of those nine
days were almost too painful to relate; but I must
put them down here, as an example of the kind of idiotic
mess one may get into, for no very apparent reason—
except, perhaps, playing about on shore, when one ought
to be getting on with a passage.

After a fast sail to the Lizard, the wind went south-west
again, and we ran before a fresh gale for more than twenty-
four hours to Milford Haven. For part of the time, the
ship was down to a small staysail, and warps were streamed
astern to slow her and avoid being pooped. Even so, she was
travelling at five knots under this rig.

At dawn on the 8th, we sighted Skokholm, and saw the
wind-streaked backs of the seas marching away from us
and bursting enormously against the black cliffs, where,
above the whiteness, rain and spray swirled in tormented
curtains. We were wet and cold and short of sleep, and felt
very glad to get in.

The boat was hove to in the lee of St Anne's Head, and
the examination steamer plunged alongside.

"Who are you?"

"*Mermaid*. Southampton to Scapa Flow." I could never
quite believe the sound of my own voice as I answered this
hail. Nor, as a rule, could our questioner.

The steamer ranged close on our weather side, and, timing it nicely, an R.N.V.R. lieutenant dropped aboard us, and followed me into the damp and dishevelled hole we called the cabin. We introduced ourselves.

"How do you do?" he said. "McKechnie is my name."

I produced our talisman, the naval message form, and some sherry.

"We've been expecting you for the past fortnight," said McKechnie. "But I must say that we didn't think that you'd arrive in this sort of weather. It has been blowing a gale here. Trees and telephone wires down. How did you manage?"

We tried to be modest, realising once more what a curious paradox it is that wind and sea look far worse from the shore than from a boat.

McKechnie was keenly interested. We must have made a welcome diversion in his already monotonous job.

"I wonder," he said, "if you would come and have some dinner with me tonight? The Mess is in a house just outside the town. I could meet you with a car at the fish dock."

"Thank you," I said warmly. "We'd love to do that!"

Of course we would love to do that! What we ought to have done was to sleep and tidy up in Dale anchorage, and then continue without further delay. Then, perhaps, Margaret would not have been hurt, nor *Mermaid* smashed up, and we might have arrived at Scrabster a fortnight sooner. But to accept an invitation to go ashore and dine in cheerful company seemed reasonable enough, after three hard days at sea.

To go ashore in Milford town meant a five-mile journey up the haven, after which we should have to pass into the trawler basin through lock gates, which were opened only for an hour on either side of the time of high water.

To get out again, we should have to move at the next opening of the gates, which was between four-thirty and six-thirty next morning. Since it would be dark at that time, we should have to anchor with the trawlers in the fairway outside until there was light enough for us to be allowed to proceed.

Unfortunately, I had not worked all this out until after we had left the examination steamer and anchored in Dale cove.

We snatched a few hours of sleep, and when we forcibly awoke ourselves at about half-past one, it was with a sense of being dragged out of heaven. The reaction had set in, and three hours' sleep had not half cured it. When we were clear of St Anne's, open to the entrance, the huge swells coming in from outside shocked us. Though the wind had probably fallen, it still seemed to blow savagely enough, as we sped up the haven. At last, we locked into the trawler basin in heavy showers of sleet, and berthed in the narrow corner north of the fish dock.

Of dinner I have only the haziest recollection. There was a journey on foot and by car; there were the introductions, the buzz of talk, all delightful with the companionship and lightheartedness of those early months of the war; but, after only two glasses of sherry, I disgraced myself during the meal by falling asleep in my chair. Then there was more driving, more walking, another brief descent into sleep, and again the rattle of an alarm clock and the turning out into blackness and wind and rain.

It was so dark that we had difficulty in finding the lock, though there were only two hundred yards to go. A tiny red lamp, apparently suspended in mid-air and frequently occulted by creeping trawlers, marked the gates.

We got into and through the lock without damage.

In the fairway outside, all was as black as the pit. Out there were dozens of anchored trawlers, their position indicated only by dim pin-points of light. I found it impossible to choose a berth properly. In what seemed a clear space, well away from the lock, we let go the anchor, with plenty of chain.

Immediately, it began to drag. Before we could get it, it stuck fast, and as we fell back on it, thinking to let well alone, we found ourselves close alongside a trawler which was showing no light whatsoever, not even a riding light. Then we realised that our anchor was almost certainly foul of the trawler's cable.

So far, so good. The trawler would be going to sea at daybreak, and when he got his anchor ours would be found hooked up in it; we would ask him kindly to pass it back, and that would be that.

Fenders were rigged, and the *Mermaid* lay easily enough alongside the trawler, both vessels head to wind and to what remained of the flood tide.

We hailed our neighbour repeatedly, and, to our surprise, getting no reply, concluded they must all be asleep.

After a couple of hours, the darkness began to be less dark, and I could dimly make out the figure of a man walking up and down the trawler's deck. I thought I had better explain and apologise as soon as possible about our anchor; and so went over the trawler's side and accosted the watchman. He regarded me with indifference. "No speak English" was his disconcerting reply.

I tried him in French. No good. He simply walked up and down, as indifferent as if he had been a German agent —which, I realised later, he very probably was.

At about this time, the *Mermaid* began to lift and pound against the great ironbound monkey-belting along the trawler's side. We put out more fenders, which were torn off one by one as the motion increased. We got boathooks and spars, and, at considerable risk of being impaled, tried to boom her off, but they were soon broken and our bulwarks began to suffer. The sentinel on the trawler's deck looked down at us from time to time. I shouted to him to get fenders, but he showed no sign of understanding.

The tide, now ebbing, was swinging the trawler broadside to wind and sea, and by ill luck we were on her windward side.

At this point I should have started the engine, let the rest of our anchor chain go, and cleared out. I suppose I was too tired to judge properly between the minor disadvantage of losing the anchor and chain and the increasing danger which threatened the ship if we tried to hang on to them. If the light had been stronger, these alternatives would have been more obvious. As it was, perhaps, I funked the idea of letting go and jilling uncertainly about under engine for another hour in the dark in a crowded anchorage (for our kedge anchor alone would not have held us).

The motion increased, as the pressure of the tide forced the trawler further round against the wind. Short, choppy seas began to fling the *Mermaid* bodily against that infernal rubbing-strake. The bulwarks on our starboard side splintered and broke away. We had nothing left with which we could fend off.

Dawn came, and—blessed relief—hands appeared on the trawler's deck and began to get the anchor.

As they did so, their cable drew slowly across our bows, and another trawler to our left sheered over towards us. Shouting now began between the two ships. It was clear that not only was *Mermaid*'s anchor foul of the first trawler's cable, but that the trawler's cable was also foul of the second trawler's gear, which was of wire.

Slowly the second ship drew close ahead. We were tied to them both. All three vessels plunged together in the rising sea, and sheets of spray flew over everything. At the top of a sudden lift the *Mermaid* seemed to be dragged forward. Her bowsprit came down with a crash on No. 2 trawler's bulwarks, and snapped short at the stem head.

"Hi!" called our watchman, coming suddenly to life, "Hi, you break your sheep!"

By this time I had got the engine going and was at the tiller, ready to back away as soon as our anchor should appear—I still clung idiotically to the notion of saving that anchor. Margaret and Kirk were forward, trying to take in our chain as No. 1 trawler hove in her cable. At last our anchor came into sight, jammed in the cable. Someone unhooked it, and it was passed aboard of us, and we were free.

As we backed out of that miserable situation, I was aware of Margaret in the cockpit beside me, saying quietly:

"I think I have hurt my hand. Would you have a look at it?"

She held it out to me in the half light—her left hand. The forefinger was gone.

It was a hundred yards or so back to the pontoon beside the lock gates, and we had to bring the boat back there before we could do anything. Then, leaving Kirk to make fast, I went below, where the lamp still burned in the cabin.

The upper half of the finger had gone, as though it had been dragged out of the joint, leaving a red stump, which scarcely bled at all.

Perhaps it was a small matter, but I had to restrain a strong impulse to be sick.

"Does it hurt you?"

"No, I can't feel anything. It was like a deep cut, at first. I was holding on to the chain with Kirk. I think a wire came across it. But it was too dark to see."

It was a mercy, I thought bitterly, that she had not lost her hand, or even her life, in that utter mess. I pulled out the medicine chest, and put a dressing on her hand.

Then I got out the rum, and we all had a stiff drink.

Kirk and I sat in silence, while the boat rocked against the staging, and through the cabin doorway the grey light showed the rain, beating upon the smashed taffrail, and the heads of stanchions sticking up round the edge of the streaming counter, like broken teeth.

"You're both very solemn!" said Margaret.

I looked at her. Her hair had come adrift from its moorings. Her feet were bare. Her old duffel coat had several large rents in it. She was soaked, as we all were, to the skin. She finished her rum, and put the mug beside her in the bunk, for the floor was still awash.

"What I'd really like now," she said, "is some breakfast!"

Kirk started the Primus, while I pumped the boat dry and checked the damage.

The smashed, splintered wood along the starboard side, and the jagged ends of the fine pitch-pine spar which had been the bowsprit, all tangled with its gear, were enough to make one sick.

Yet, perhaps it was not really so bad. The mess looked horrible. But on close examination it all boiled down to bowsprit and bulwarks, and one bent rigging screw. I checked everything as carefully as the prevailing conditions allowed, and, as far as I could see, there was really nothing else the matter.

We fed, and felt better; and I went ashore to look for a car and a doctor. Margaret then went off to Haverfordwest hospital to have the finger properly tidied up; and Kirk and I set ourselves to have the ship repaired in as short a time as possible.

All that day, we tramped the docks and the town, finding someone—anyone—who was able and could be persuaded to tackle our various jobs. We improved the occasion by raising petrol—by dint of spinning our threadbare yarn many times in many offices—and carried the drums in relays from a garage a mile away.

We decided, while we had the chance, to have six feet cut off the boom, and to rig twin topping-lifts. A long train of enquiry led at last to a sailmaker, who promised to re-cut the leach of the mainsail to suit the shortened boom. And after we had locked in again to our former berth, we marked a great store of motor tyres—the only type of fender which was of the slightest use to us—festooned along the sides of a lighter, and lifted a dozen of them after dark. We were learning to live on the country!

The next evening, I went to Haverfordwest in the bus, bearing chocolates and apples, to see Margaret.

As soon as I went in she ran out to meet me, dressed as I had left her (except that her clothes were dry) and announced that she was coming back with me forthwith.

"I'm not staying here any longer. I'm perfectly all right. The nurse wouldn't give me back my clothes this morning, but I found them. You'll have to cope with Matron, or she'll have my life. Food! Bless you! I'm *very* hungry."

I left her taking in nourishment, whilst I went in search of surgical opinion. Dr Williams had amputated her finger the previous night under a general anaesthetic, in order to be able to cover the bone properly. He had heard something of our tale from Margaret. "Let her take it easy for a while," he said. "Leave the dressing alone for ten days, unless there's any pain. No, no charge! Good luck!"

We returned to the ship, feeling better than we had felt since the smash. Margaret was resolved to come on with the ship to Dunlaoire. We made a bargain, therefore, that she should spend Christmas with her people in Ireland, whilst Kirk and I would try to shanghai one of the Dublin yachtsmen to take the boat on, and she would rejoin us in Scotland. That night, with all arrangements in train, we slept like the dead.

The week flashed past, in days full of tramping, diplomacy, cajolery, occasional curses, and hours of list-making and carpentry and rigger's work. Another gale came and went. McKechnie, with relays of his friends, boarded us at intervals and cheered us on. He asked us to report any foreign trawlers we might meet in the Irish Sea, since a little party of refugee fishermen, who had been enjoying the hospitality of Brixham, had just been discovered arranging roof-light beacons for the guidance of German bombers towards Plymouth and Bristol.

At last, all was shipshape, and on the morning of the 17th December we said good-bye, and motored once more out of the dock.

Mermaid did not enter it again for five years—until, in the autumn of 1945, Margaret and I brought her there again on her way south and tied her up in her old corner.

By that time, a good deal more had happened to her, and her work was done.

5

IN TUAS MANUS

"But sea-room, an the brine and cloudy billow
kiss the moon, I care not."

Pericles

SAILING in the dead of winter can be lovelier than in
high summer. The days were so short that much of my
memory of that journey from Milford to Inverness is
of the starlit night—what Stevenson must have had in
mind when he wished to be buried "under the wide and
starry sky" and what the French describe with their inimit-
able gift for phrase, as living "à la belle étoile".

Soon after four o'clock the sun would go down red behind
his frost curtain, and for an hour or so the islands would
lie like black bubbles on the rim of the sea. Then the old
snow-grained heads of the hills would blaze westward in
final obeisance before the orange colour drained away into
the dead greys and duns of the twilight, soon to turn to
black and silver as the moon and the stars took charge.

As the frost thickened, the stars seemed to snap and
crackle overhead. On Christmas Eve their reflections
looked up from the black, still water of the little basin at
Ardrishaig upon three contented mariners replete with a
Christmas dinner of jugged hare and plum pudding, which
Kirk had produced miraculously on a couple of Primus
stoves. When one of the three, Keith McFerran, from the
Royal St George Yacht Club at Dunlaoire, who was helping
us in Margaret's place, left four days later at Banavie, the
stars were still shining through cloudless and windless
nights, until the mercury shrank into its bulb, the canal
froze, and metal became tacky and dangerous to the touch.

44

They were still there, in the dawn, supporting a pale emerald moon, when the *Mermaid* dropped her ice-plates at Fort Augustus and, with scored sides and ropes as stiff as bars, stepped between mist and water into Loch Ness. At Inverness their quiet reign was broken. After two days' work on the ship we put out past Fort George, and there came a grey sky and a short chop from the east to remind us that we were once more in the open sea.

We sailed into Invergordon just before sunset, with the feeling that for us that lovely harbour was the last soft spot on earth.

The *Mermaid* had brought us safely many miles. There were only a hundred or so left to go, but the final lap was a proposition which I viewed without the least enthusiasm. Perhaps I was soft and spoiled from easy living during the past fortnight in sheltered waters, but it certainly seemed to me that the passage from Invergordon to Scrabster was not one to be attempted in the middle of winter in a forty-foot sailing boat of doubtful soundness, unless one could choose one's time. Choosing time was the one thing we could not do. We were overdue, and we had to get on.

As dusk fell, we tied up to a pontoon below the town, and, when we had made ourselves presentable, Kirk and I went ashore to report. As usual, when calling at a naval base, there was the fear that we should not be allowed to go on; but at Naval Control, Kirk met an old acquaintance, Captain Carpenter, who, having heard our tale, proceeded to frank us to the end of our journey. He invited us, if the weather was wrong, to dine with him the following night at the R.N. Club.

Next day, we woke to find everything beyond the ship shrouded in drifts of cold North Sea fog. Naval Control told us that further north it was blowing hard and that Wick harbour was inaccessible—news which gave me a kind of miserable relief.

We unrolled the chart and settled down in *Mermaid*'s cabin to review the problem. It fell into two parts—the approach to the Pentland Firth, and the passage through it.

The approach, from Invergordon to Duncansby Head, the eastern gate of the Firth, was eighty miles long. In that stretch there was only one refuge, the artificial harbour of Wick, a fishing town twenty miles short of Duncansby. It was a very doubtful refuge, since it was inaccessible in any onshore wind amounting to a strong breeze. Therefore, if the wind blew strongly from the east, we should be on a lee shore, and should either have to ride it out or run back to Invergordon. To ride it out might require an offing of at least fifteen miles, and running back to Invergordon would be a protracted business if we had got far to the north before it blew up.

Now for the Firth. To enable us to pass through it, two conditions were essential. We must arrive at Duncansby at the beginning of the ebb or west-going tide; and there must be no west wind nor even a westerly swell in the Firth itself.

At the moment, we had been told, there was a fresh east wind blowing to the north. The area of this wind probably extended to the Firth, and would cut any drain of swell resulting there from previous westerly gales. So far, so good.

The question was, would this east wind pipe up to gale force? We were getting uncomfortably near the season for the spring easterlies, those black winds out of the steppes, that rage for days on end. Well, we should see.

For the next day or two, the favourable tide began at Duncansby during the forenoon and late evening. In order to pass the Firth in daylight we would have to use the forenoon tide, and make our passage northwards during the previous night.

During the afternoon, we shopped and did small jobs about the ship; and soon after dark we tidied up and went to meet our host.

Our awakening next morning, Sunday the 7th January,

was of that slow, stertorous kind, which results from too much acceptance of hospitality the day before. I felt distinctly the worse for wear, as I rolled out of the warm blankets, hooked back the door of the cockpit, and looked out upon a whitened world.

There was about an inch of snow on deck. Hills and sky were almost of the same dead colour. The air was bitingly cold. There was not a breath of wind at sea level, but, high up, pale ranks of stratus cloud were moving very slowly from the east.

As the keen air and the beauty of the place woke me up, I realised that it was a fine morning, and that we should probably have to sail.

At breakfast, we decided that if the forecast was for a continuance of the strong east wind further north, we would not sail until it moderated. If for a west wind, we would go up to Wick and wait there for a change. If, on the other hand, the forecast was for moderate easterly winds and settled weather for the next twenty-four hours, we would try to do the whole run to Scrabster. We would sail at midday, jill along quietly through the night, and aim to be at Duncansby Head at daylight to catch the first of the west-going tide.

After breakfast I went up to the Control office, and, after looking at the forecast, which was good, I said that we would go. One of our hosts of the previous evening was on duty, and he promised to signal the entrance forts and the examination vessel, and wished us luck. I felt we were going to need it!

There was so little breeze in the harbour that we had to motor to the entrance, but as we cleared the Sutors a bitter wind from the south-east pressed the boat down, and we braced ourselves to face the beam sea and the gathering dusk.

The tide being still fair and the wind freshening with the dark, we went quickly up the straight piece of coast to Tarbet Ness. Following our usual custom in these conditions, we hove to at nightfall and pulled down all three reefs.

Margaret took the first watch, for I wanted to be on deck when we passed Clyth Ness, the light on the north side, which provides a kind of landfall for a vessel crossing the wide mouth of the Dornoch Firth. At eleven-thirty she called me, to say that, by reckoning, we should be abeam of Clyth Ness, but that she could see nothing of the light. It was evidently not working.

Just at this time, the wind was blowing about Force 6, a stiff breeze that put the ship down to her covering board, even with three reefs in her mainsail, and kept her heaving and dropping, with considerable turmoil, in the beam sea. She would stand a bit more, but not much, on this course. The thought that consumed me was that we were on a lee shore, which was unlit and shelterless.

In these circumstances, I began to let the ship run up to windward. With the wind abeam, and only a small jib set forward, the tiller pulled strongly at my arms. As she rose to each wave, she tried to point her nose towards it, and I let her edge up, for that moment, only pulling her back to her proper course as the wave passed beneath her. Thus, for half the time, her head was to windward of the course I had set, and she was slowly creeping off the land.

This was all very well. I was gaining sea room, in case the wind should increase. I did not sufficiently bear in mind that we should have to enter the Pentland Firth, that is, be close off Duncansby Head, not later than ten-thirty in the morning.

And now two further factors combined to prevent our keeping this most essential appointment.

Kirk came up at four a.m., and I told him what I had done during my watch. I went below and marked our position, finding that the estimated half point I had allowed to windward had put us, in four hours of smart sailing, rather far off the land. But this anxious night was coming to an end; we had nearly travelled our distance, and I comforted myself with the thought that, when we had done so, we could run in very quickly, with the wind behind us, to the mouth of the Firth.

However, we had no such luck. At five o'clock the wind fell away completely. And at the same time the tide began to pour eastwards out of the mouth of the Firth, setting the ship further away into the North Sea. With the dread of the onshore wind now replaced by the dread of missing our mark, we started the motor and turned the ship's head towards the land.

Daylight came slowly, with a dull haar that reduced visibility to two or three miles. There was no sign of land. The wind had died, the tide had us in its grip, and it was five hours before there loomed ahead a line of overhanging stacks and cliffs, which were identified as Staxigeo. We were fifteen miles south of Duncansby; the tide was past its turn; and even with its help we should reach the mouth of the Firth in this light air two hours behind schedule. That would mean that we should not get through until it changed again and stopped us short of our destination as effectively as a lock gate.

There was nothing for it but to go into Wick.

We made a meal, and felt a little better. Although I was ashamed of myself for the over-caution which had caused us to miss the bus, I was sufficiently content with the thought of having advanced our base to Wick, only twenty miles from the east gate of the Firth. We had written off sixty miles of the unsheltered approach, and the final run from Wick would require only a few hours of suitable weather.

At one o'clock in that grey day, the dark little roofs and towers of Wick appeared drearily enough beyond the swells in an angle of low cliffs, white with bursting surf.

The swells seemed to us to be very large as we motored gingerly towards the mouth of the bay. They rode easily beneath the ship, but, as they ran in ahead of us, they heaved monstrously, and there blew and wheeled above them what appeared to be droves of white seabirds, but we saw, as we moved nearer, that these were gouts of foam. Evidently the ground shelved and shallowed very much in this little notch of the coast.

Evidently, too, there had been more wind than we had thought during the night. Now, as we tried to pick up the entrance, we could see the swell bursting white all along the harbour-front before the town in an unbroken line. There was no gap in the break to indicate where the entrance was.

I was busy below with the Pilot Book when Kirk called me on deck. We had been uncertain which of the miscellaneous buildings was the coastguard station referred to in the book. There was no doubt about it now. From a low silhouette, like that of a fort, to the left of the town, black shapes were rising to the head of a flagstaff. I checked with the book. It was the signal that the harbour was inaccessible. We could not go in.

I am sorry to say that although in after days I met many delightful "Wickers", no amount of acquaintance ever improved my first impression of that God-forgotten little town. There would have been light for us in it, even so, more than in fairy cities, if it would have let us in. But the swell, that did no more than rock us where we lay, was piling up and gathering speed in the shallow water, until, at the harbour mouth, it would have turned the boat end over end. Robert Louis Stevenson describes somewhere how the attempt to build a proper breakwater at Wick was the one great failure of his father's life.

Sick at heart, we turned round against the inset of the swell and motored back to sea. There were two things we could do—go back to Invergordon, or spend the night dodging on and off the coast until the morning.

In deciding to wait another twenty hours for the morning tide, we were simply taking the kind of chance which, now and then, we would have to take, if we were to get anywhere. But I firmly believe it was the longest chance we ever did take, either before, or afterwards, when we were crossing the Firth itself with full cargoes.

It was a bet on the weather. There would have been little in it—or not so much—if the *Mermaid* had been capable of riding out a gale in the short steep seas of that place. But I did not think she was. We could not even give ourselves proper sea room, because, if the wind held light, there would be a repetition of the morning's performance. If it blew, there could be no question of clawing off shore. No boat of *Mermaid*'s size and shape would make headway against a gale and short seas—we had had a demonstration of that at Brixham. We had to stay close to the position we would need to be in next morning. If the wind blew, it would blow us on to the rocks.

In succeeding winters at Scrabster, when it blew three full-powered gales from three different points inside two days, or when the wind raged blackly out of the east for fifteen days at a stretch, we used to think of that quiet January night we spent between Wick and Duncansby, somewhere off Noss Head—on the edge of eternity.

It did not blow more than a deathly, questing air, that slapped and whined amongst the rigging. The watchkeeper, bunched against the cockpit coaming, would see not even a kindly glow from the skylight, which was blacked out, but only the binnacle, the beginnings of spars, the ghostly mass of the mainsail, and the baleful gleams overside, where the tops of seas broke like the snarl of wolves. He would cheer the numb envelope of the flesh with biscuits and raisins, whilst the small flame of his spirit communed with the great sibilant night-drift which surrounded him.

Interminably the darkness seemed to hold, and even, in the dead hours before the dawn, to thicken.

Watch succeeded watch: alternating periods, when the core of life, ever calculating, speculating, wondering, hoping, hung in the cold bourne like the prophet's coffin, or lay, still conscious—if slightly warmer—beneath veils of uneasy sleep. The minutes, which seemed so leaden, consumed themselves at their even pace, and in its time the light grew.

From four in the morning the tide had been against us, and we had been partly stemming it—short tacks out, long tacks in. But for fifteen hours we had swum in a black void. We had been on this tack or on that tack; the little needle of the log had turned so far round its dial after such and such an expiration of time; and upon the chart, pinned to a board in the spare bunk, there had accumulated a clump of pencilled zig-zag lines, each ending in a circle and a figure, which denoted the hopeful mariner's idea of his position at the end of each blind manœuvre.

At last, the light came, and showed us the coast.

It lay, as we had hoped it would, not far to the west of us. It appeared first as a mass only slightly darker than the smoky haze which wreathed it. Then we saw brows of stone overhanging lifting lips of white, where the swells burst and spouted in the chimneys. Certain masses detached themselves from this background: great mushroom-like towers of black shale slabs, that leaned outwards threateningly towards the swells that charged in upon them.

This must be Sinclair Bay. We were only eight miles from Duncansby, and it was barely eight o'clock. The glass was still high and steady. The wind had veered a little towards the south. It blew fresh and raw, but it was a dawn wind and it held no terrors for us.

We shook the reefs out of the mainsail, set our big jib, and pointed up along the coast, sure this time of keeping our appointment. The last of the flood, setting down along the coast from the Firth, made a jobble of sea in that long riffle known as the Bores of Duncansby; but it would ease and flatten with the change of tide, and we barged into it with light hearts and an appetite for breakfast that its dying fury could not impair.

Just before we reached Duncansby, a trawler going south passed close, plunging deep into the seas, and waved cheerfully. Then there rose on our left the overhanging nose, three hundred feet high, with the white lighthouse on its summit braying mournfully into empty haze beyond. It was the end of the land, the east gate of the Pentland Firth.

Humbly, we crept round the foot of it, in deep water just clear of the backwash of the bursting swells, and turned westwards into a misty sea.

To the right, nothing was visible. To the left, a low coastline presently fell away southwards. Our course lay towards the distant point of St John's. The ebb tide, hitting that point, was deflected by it into the Atlantic in a great stickle, seven or eight miles long at mid-tide, which, if it met any swell or wind from the west, reared into an impassable sea—the race called the Men of Mey.

We looked anxiously ahead as the strengthening tide swept us westwards. But all the sea was calm; even the easterly swell had died as soon as we rounded Duncansby. In the absence of any wind from the west to strengthen it, the westerly swell, which drains in eternally from the Atlantic, is cut and driven back at every tide by the outpouring of water through the Firth. Tide and sea would be peaceful forces if they had not the wind to raise the devil in them!

As we approached St John's, another great headland rose beyond it in the haze. It seemed so far away that for a moment we had difficulty in believing that we must pass it to reach Scrabster. Sea and weather were quiet, but this, our first passage of the Firth, was for me an edgy business, and I wanted to get in.

With an hour of tide still in our favour, we found ourselves sliding past the headland, which was a long bastion of great cliffs with a lighthouse on top at the outer edge of the curve.

As we came abreast of it, the cliffs fell away in a magnificent recession, displaying a wide bay, with a little town set in the midst of low shores, like a town in a Dutch picture; though this one was guarded by a tower that stood to the left, black and lonely, at the edge of the surf.

Far back, behind vast sweeps of moor, lay the tops of mountains, conical, like extinct volcanoes, white with snow.

The haze had cleared sufficiently to allow bars of yellow light to glow in the west, but the daylight was beginning to fail, and we could not for some time see anything in the south-west corner of the bay, towards which we were heading. From that point a bluff of low cliffs ran out a mile or so to the main waters of the Firth, and all beneath it was in black shadow. The wind had died; and now we were out of the full set of the tide, so that it was an hour before we could discern, deep in the angle of the bay, a tiny glimmer of white cottages showing dimly at the edge of the water.

In time we saw a quay wall. We slowed down, and moved onwards quietly on an even keel, the dusk deepening, and the air of approaching night cold on our faces. We felt like children who were coming home; for beyond the entrance we could now see the shapes of houses, a little blank-looking without the lighted windows of peacetime, but built and lived-in by people.

Then we were gliding between pier-heads of dark stone into a tiny harbour.

6

A PLAY TOWARD

"What hempen homespuns have we swaggering here,
So near the cradle of the fairy queen?"
A Midsummer Night's Dream

A VOICE hailed, and hailed again. The sharp, urgent hail from the deck, that meant: "Turn out and fight!"—that switched on consciousness as inevitably as a switch turns on current: current, just now, from a rather faded battery!

There was daylight in the cabin, and it was the white daylight that is reflected from snow. The air coming in through a crack of opening in the skylight was cold and clean.

But something had gone wrong somewhere. In the doorway there crouched a man whom I knew very well, but whom I had last seen on the deck of a neighbouring yacht during a race to Bremerhaven. He was dressed in soldier's uniform; and he was saying, in a tone of voice in which cheerfulness was not unmixed, it seemed to me, with anxiety:

"Tony, you old so-and-so, what are you doing here?"

I raised myself on an elbow, and regarded this apparition.

"Tarrant," I said, "is that you? And, if it is you, why are you disguised as a soldier? And what, by the same token, are *you* doing in Scrabster?"

"I'm a military policeman, old boy. There's a certain amount of excitement about you. I was supposed to escort you to N.O.I.C. about an hour ago, but I thought you'd probably be needing some rest."

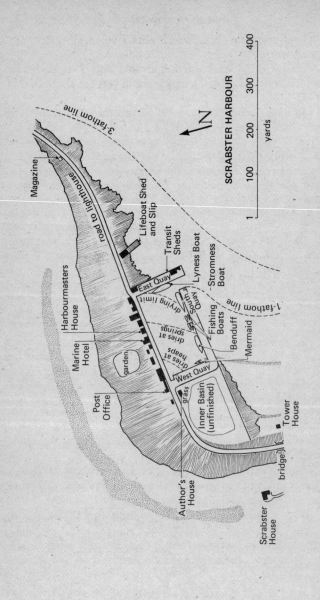

SCRABSTER HARBOUR

3-fathom line

Magazine

road to lighthouse

Lifeboat Shed
and Slip

Transit
Sheds

East Quay

Lyness Boat

Stromness
Boat

Harbourmasters
House

drying limit

South Quay

1-fathom line

Marine Hotel

garden

Fishing
Boats

Benduff

Mermaid

dries at springs

Post Office

dries at heaps

West Quay

grass

Author's House

Inner Basin
(unfinished)

Tower House

bridge

Scrabster House

N

100   200   300   400

yards

1

"Good morning, Bill," came Kirk's voice, sleepily. "It's a small world!"

"Good God!" exclaimed Tarrant, and I thought he sounded relieved. "How many more of you are there in this vessel?"

"Only me," said Margaret. "Did you think we'd come to blow up the Fleet?"

"Well, as a matter of fact, you've given us quite a turn. Small white yacht reported the day before yesterday trying to get into Wick. Reported yesterday passing through the Firth, not answering signals. This is a prohibited area, you know, and—to be quite frank—there's an idea of sending you home. What are you up to?"

We explained. Tarrant heard us with amusement, tempered with the reserve proper to his new calling and to the fact that he might shortly be called upon to put us under arrest. He would not stay for coffee—it was past ten o'clock—and turned to leave, telling us to report to N.O.I.C. that evening.

"Who is N.O.I.C., Thurso?" Kirk enquired. "What's he like?"

"Captain Norton—'Peg-Leg' Norton," replied Tarrant. "Wooden leg. Bluff and hearty. Not a bad sort of chap."

Through the mists of departing sleep the name rang a bell in my mind, and I thought that wonders would never cease. "Bill," I said, "do you happen to know if Norton comes from a place called Dalwhinnie?"

"Yes, I believe his home is there. Why? Do you know him?"

"If he's the man I'm thinking of, I've met him, shooting, with an uncle of mine. Bill, he's not going to send us home! You don't get rid of us as easily as that!"

"Well, I hope not. But watch your step! I'll be seeing you tonight."

It was an anxious party that busied itself with break-fast. We began to see that we had arrived only upon the threshold of new and far greater difficulties than wind and tide; and so absorbed did we become in the pros and cons of our situation that we had finished our meal and tidied the cabin before we thought of having a look round outside.

The tide was at half ebb, so that we had to climb on to the quay by means of the light-boards in the shrouds. Then the place lay clear about us, sunshine and snow making bright and near all that had been dark the previous evening.

Thurso Bay is a great kidney-shaped scoop in the north coast of Caithness. Scrabster lies on the western lobe of the bay, tucked under an outjutting ridge, which ends in Holburn Head. The village is simply a single line of cottages—there is no room for more—strung along the foot of this ridge. It faces nearly south. The ridge is a very steep grassy slope about a hundred feet high, produced by an erosion of the sea, which had been too gentle, in that sheltered corner, to make a cliff of it. South of the village, it makes a rather abrupt turn eastward, and at that point the village road climbs a little on the curving face before dipping away along the shore towards Thurso.

The harbour is simply a rectangle, about two hundred yards by a hundred, lying in front of the village. The outer wall (on which the *Mermaid* lay) was continued across the corner, enclosing a large pond which had been proposed as an inner basin but never finished—later on, we were to wish heartily that it had been! The east quay, sticking out from the seaward end of the village, was the berthing place for the Lyness steamers. The wall on which we lay provided the only other deep-water berths.

Looking east across the bay from where we stood, we could see, to the left of Thurso, the tower which had been such a landmark to us the day before. Beyond it, a wide arm of the bay ran south-east again, and from the far side of this eastern lobe there grew and marched back into the middle distance the great convex rampart of Dunnet Head, its flat-topped line of three-hundred-foot cliffs looming opposite Scrabster across a four-mile stretch of sea as though it were the far side of a pond.

The sea shone unbroken, but a long, slow breath beneath the surface spent itself along the ledges towards Thurso in a continual murmur. The water beneath our feet was like a sheet of clear glass. The air was angel-pure, cold and sparkling like an intoxicating draught. All this northern world was so huge and fresh that in it one seemed to have been reborn.

"Nice day! Did ye sleep?" It was the small man who had taken our lines the night before. He had a weathered face, a moustache of the kind permitted to merchant captains of a past generation, and blue eyes that twinkled like a boy's.

"We certainly did, Captain Shearer!"

"I must move ye up a bit. The Stromness boat berths here in the deep watter, and that's the *Benduff*'s berth ahead of her. I left ye here last night so 'at ye wouldn't tak the ground. But I'm afraid ye'll have to lie on the west quay. Ye'll be clear o' a' boaties there."

For the next quarter-of-an-hour, he helped us to tow gently along the south quay, across the angle, and into a new berth on the west quay. We elicited the devastating fact that we should take the ground at low water for several days during spring tides. As we were soon to learn, the entire harbour dried in certain conditions, with the exception only of a pool at the entrance, into which the Lyness steamer, the *St Ninian*, could poke but half her length if her schedule happened to coincide with the time of low water.

Sounding with a boathook showed that we would be on the ground in our new berth in a few minutes, so we delayed a proposed expedition to Thurso in order to see the ship safely down.

Grounding a deep-keeled boat, like a small yacht, that cannot lie on her bilges, is a tricky business. The list must be just right: not too much, or the main rigging will catch the edge of the wall; not too little, or the ship may fall outwards and fill as the tide comes back. The boom must be placed far enough across to give the ship this list, but not so far as to catch on the edge of the quay as she goes down. Finally, the warps at bow and stern must be turned up at exactly such a length as to bring the ship close alongside the wall at the moment she touches the ground. In the course of the next three years, we did all these things several hundred times: it was a demanding occupation!

Once the boat was well on the ground, it was safe to leave her until the ensuing low water.

We had only to walk a few yards up the quay, at which *Mermaid* now lay, to reach the road at the Post Office, which was the first of the single line of cottages comprising the village. Here, the previous evening, I had sent a telegram to let Harrison know we had arrived.

We turned left along the road, walked up the long slope, and soon opened a vision of the snow-covered cliffs of Hoy that filled the seaward horizon. To the east, they ran as far as we could see and disappeared, hull down, beyond Dunnet. To the west, as we opened them further, they rose steadily, until, coming clear of Holburn Head, they were cut off abruptly, like the bows of a vast battleship. It was an appalling termination—eleven hundred feet of rock, very nearly sheer, fronting proudly the dominions of the North Atlantic.

"What a place!" said Margaret quietly. "That ought to be Ultima Thule—not Shetland. Well, boys—not long now!"

We speculated about our course across the Firth, which would lie on a slant to the north-east, where the island was lower. And so, red in the face from cold and excitement and brisk walking, we came to Thurso, which we found to be a small stone-built town, not much bigger than a large village. set amongst fields between the sea and the mouth of the little Thurso River.

All the country lay in long sweeps, which ran down or

rose in close-cropped grass to bluffs or high cliffs at the sea, and, inland, became tracts of heather and peat.

Walking the streets and doing bits of shopping was, for once, a luxury. But the crown and summit was a hot bath at the St Magnus Hotel. We drank coffee afterwards in a lounge, where there were one or two naval officers, a larger sprinkling of wives, and a few civilians, who did not bear the stamp of locals and who belonged to the swelling tide of contractors and engineers which was flowing north to re-fortify the islands.

I forget the details of what we did during the remainder of that day, until the time came for our interview with N.O.I.C. But I know that it was filled with an infinity of small businesses, and that it became the pattern for almost every succeeding day that we had to spend in Thurso.

Up to this time, our work had been confined in space to the ship, and, for her maintenance and ours, to a relatively small radius ashore whenever we touched port. Now, although the ship needed even more attention, owing to her distracting necessity of continually taking the ground, we had the new factor of cargo to consider. There was petrol to see to—a very knotty problem. We had to find a lorry to carry the explosives from the station, and to look for sources of supply for ship's gear. And there were Customs officers to be met and gauged. All this, at the moment, was tentative, because its condition was the sanction of the naval authorities, who controlled everything.

At about four o'clock, having returned to Scrabster, fussed over the ship, and watched the Lyness mailboat come in—an ancient, narrow steamer, with raked masts and funnel, as conventional as a Victorian postcard—we arrayed ourselves with care, and climbed into the St Magnus Hotel bus, to go to Thurso again for our interview with N.O.I.C.

Margaret was cheerful; Kirk, in his blue overcoat and trilby hat, reserved and much the most respectable; while

I, full of the justice of our cause, clasped a red cardboard folder containing our three documents.

We tried to relax, rather unsuccessfully, over drinks and a meal in the hotel; concluded that innocence and a modest enthusiasm would be the best approach; and then, the tension growing in our throats, walked up the frosty street to Naval Control.

N.O.I.C. and his staff had commandeered a place called Airlie House, a large private house on the landward side of the town, near the station. We gave our names to a steward, and were conducted to a room where Norton, Tarrant, and a Marine captain, of plethoric habit, were drinking coffee in front of a fire.

"These people," said Norton jovially, introducing us to the Marine, "arrived here last night in a boat about the size of that sofa—to carry dynamite across to Orkney, if you please!—Where did you come from, Bridges?— Southampton?—Can't help thinking the best thing to do would be to send 'em home!"

The Marine cast an eye over our crumpled flannels and reefers without enthusiasm. He took up, at the point where our entry had interrupted it, a narrative of how a gunner in his command had shot down a German bomber in a recent raid on the Flow.

A Wren officer came in, and gave us coffee. The Marine turned his story over and over, as though the bomber had been a grouse in a gale, and his gunner a good dog. Eventually the replication of detail filled him to the point of silence, and a question-mark began to grow and spread itself in our direction.

Bill Tarrant sat watching us while we gave an account of ourselves. I think he tumbled to us fairly quickly, for he knew us all well. Norton was more difficult. He did not sail, for one thing; and it was evident from the outset that, in spite of previous acquaintance, he had to be treated carefully by a party of amateur yachtsmen with nothing to show for themselves but a naval message form (now rather the worse for wear), a *transire*, and some letters of a commercial nature.

Probably I underestimated, as usual, the difficulties we presented to those whom we asked to take responsibility for letting us loose. In those days it seemed to me an unnecessary waste of time to have to ask at all to be allowed to help in the war, particularly when we asked nothing that we were not prepared to pay for—or try to pay for—out of our own pockets. I could have borne being told that we were an embarrassment; I was even prepared to sit up and beg, to almost any extent; but to be questioned closely about my motives was a thing that pressed me hard. I did not know at that time that there was a spy scare in Orkney; or appreciate sufficiently what my own reactions, as responsible officer, would have been, had two men and a girl asked me to authorise them to enter a fleet anchorage with four tons of high explosive in a small yacht. The upshot was, that after an hour or more of cross-examination I delivered myself as follows:

"Look, sir, we didn't come nine hundred miles in a forty-foot boat in the dead of winter to this God-forgotten place for any other purpose than to do a job of work, which we understood required to be done, and for which *all* of us have certain qualifications. I don't give a damn who carries this stuff across to Orkney"—(play it wide open, I thought!) —"so long as it *is* carried. But, since we put in for the job when no one else did, and were allowed to fit out a boat at our own expense and spend a month getting here in order to do it, we feel that, whoever does it, we have at least earned the right to try!"

There was silence for some time. Tarrant was grinning. Norton and the Marine were slightly flushed; and I wondered if I had completely upset the apple-cart.

It was Tarrant who came to our rescue with some quiet remark; and, soon afterwards, the inquisition broke up. Tarrant saw us to the door, and murmured hopeful words to us as we departed.

We three walked home by torchlight, and Margaret and I blew off steam all the way back to Scrabster. Kirk, older and wiser than either of us, took a more rational view of Norton's reactions, and eventually persuaded us that our outfit was, after all, by 1914 standards, a little unusual.

The next morning I had to write out a statement of our case for Norton to forward to A.C.O.S., the Admiral Commanding Orkneys and Shetlands. I put all I had into it. The result was rather long, but it was complete and it stated the case. I wrote it out in a fair round hand and left it at Airlie Lodge.

Later in the day, a telegram arrived from Harrison: "Wire received. Wrote you yesterday. Despatching 200 boxes (5 tons) explosives to your order at Thurso. Delivery Lyness expected during week 22/29 January."

Delivery was *expected*. I should think it was—we were a fortnight late already. It was now the 10th January. The consignment would probably take a week to travel from Wales. We should at any rate have time to make all preparations for the first trip.

Mrs Maclaren, at the Post Office, was a cheerful and kindly soul. She had a small, square, stone house, very like all the others, and it had a bathroom and a couple of spare bedrooms. Being already £90 in debt, we felt we could not yet afford to rent one of the bedrooms; but she kindly gave us permission to stow our spare gear in a tiny outhouse hewn out of the rock at the back. Bill Harcus, the coxswain of the lifeboat, lent us a handcart, which was used in summer for the salmon fishers' nets; and next day we sorted out, unloaded, and stowed everything we would not need. There must have been the best part of a ton of spare sails, spars, ropes, "yacht" fenders, and so on.

Then we tackled the ballast. We had been told the ship had four tons of iron bars in her. My idea was to take out about half of this, and leave a "spine" on either side of the kelson for stability. We had no means of weighing or calculating, and had to go by eye and sense. We unscrewed the

skylight, unbent the head of the mainsail, rove a whip at
the gaff end, took up the planks of the cabin floor, and
hoisted out the black, greasy pigs and furnace bars with a
wire sling. When the pile on the quay looked about the
same size as the amount left in the ship, we guyed the boom
right out, and two of us sat at the end of it, while the third
surveyed the result from every angle and groped towards a
conclusion.

People came and watched us—fishermen from the Wick
boats, Naval Control officers from the harbourmaster's
house, and, very soon, Norton himself and some of his staff.
We felt more than ever like a parcel of lunatics; but we
worked diligently under this supervision, explaining whenever we had to, refusing offers of help, and trying to look
as if we knew what we were doing.

On the 17th, the gunpowder van arrived at Thurso. I
reported to Norton, and I think he realised by this time
that we meant business. By the 19th, he had wrung a most
reluctant permission from A.C.O.S. and had sent down to
us a charming letter of personal introduction to the
Admiral, who turned out to be an old acquaintance of
Margaret's people in Ireland. I reflected sourly that if we
could continue to produce a relation or an acquaintance in
every port, we should some day be allowed to get on with
some work.

I was still having difficulty in arranging for lorries,
which were fully occupied with naval stores.

That morning, I had to see Norton, just before lunch,
and he said he would have the stuff run down to Scrabster
that afternoon. He also promised us the help of the duty
drifter's crew to help load the ship.

Urgent as the matter was, this was a little premature.
I had reckoned on a clear day to load in, because I was
not sure how the stowage would go and wanted to take my
time over it. However, I had not the face to ask for more
time, but rang up Margaret and told her to clear the cabin
and get the skylight off.

Kirk and I lunched hurriedly in the St Magnus. As we finished our coffee, I was looking out of the window at a blankness of falling snow; and suddenly I saw the naval lorry go past, loaded with boxes.

"There's our stuff," I said. "Come on, we'd better go down."

We were infinitely warm and comfortable in our chairs in the hotel lounge. We were weary with goings to and fro, and with the strain of the delay, the uncertainty, and the approaching effort. Now, we should have to change our clothes again—we were continually changing our clothes—and load cases late into the darkness. The day was already drawing in, and it was snowing hard and bitterly cold. I knew exactly what Kirk meant when he said: "Tony, be reasonable!"

I couldn't be reasonable. There was not much reason in this thing—or in the war, for that matter.

We caught the bus down to the harbour. The lorry was alongside *Mermaid*'s berth. The crew of the *Calliopsis*, the duty drifter, were handing the boxes off into a stack in the snow on the edge of the quay. In the oblong of *Mermaid*'s skylight, into which snowflakes fell, we could see Margaret, desperately trying to finish the clearing of the cabin.

Kirk and I changed somehow in the fo'c'sle; and then, for the next three hours, we passed, placed, and replaced a hundred and twenty fifty-pound boxes of gelignite, until they fitted, like a jigsaw puzzle, in a solid immovable stack in *Mermaid*'s cabin.

We hung a riding-light in the rigging, so that we could see to pass the boxes from the quay to the deck; and, below, we worked by the light of torches. We should have to light a lamp below decks sooner or later, but we thought that could wait until our helpers had departed.

When we had finished, the boxes overflowed the bunks and made a level floor in the cabin three feet high. They looked much less in bulk than they had appeared on the lorry, and there was plenty of room for more. But there was quite enough of them, we thought, for a trial trip.

I took the *Calliopsis*'s people up to the Marine, the little hotel on the quay, for a drink; and returned to find Kirk nursing a Primus with infinite care in the fo'c'sle. The snow had stopped, the glass was steady and fairly high, and it was a quiet, cold night.

We supped wearily and uncomfortably, jammed close beside one another amongst the mass of gear in the fo'c'sle, our nerves strung with the upheaval and excitement.

Afterwards, Margaret and I went out and pulled down three reefs in the frozen mainsail. I argued that it was better to do this long and tedious job in harbour than have to do it in a hurry in the Firth. If the reefs were not needed, it would be a simple matter to shake them out.

At last we turned in. Where I lay in the quarter berth, I could see the end of the stack of gelignite protruding from the cabin door beside my head, like the snout of a glacier. My final thought, as I let go into unconsciousness, was that if it went off in the night it would not worry me at all!

7

UNDER ENGINE

"Which, much enforced, shows a hasty spark,
And straight is cold again."

DARKNESS—and the smell of snow! Stars in a black
sky. Black water; black, icy stonework of the quay.
New-fallen snow thick on the deck, blurring the fittings to a ghostly outline, icing the ropes, so that the
Mermaid seemed a dead, forgotten thing, a ship for a Rip
van Winkle. Biting air—quiet, but questing from the
north-east, like a hound at check: a snow wind!

It is eighteen miles from the harbour to the point of
Switha Island. Not much; but out there, in a few hours'
time, the tide will be running like a river. What will this
wind do? Will it rise up and stamp on us? Will it blank
out everything in snow? We should never get there by dead
reckoning, sailing blind—not in the *Mermaid*, across an
eight-knot tide.

The ship was on the ground, the water a long way below
her waterline. We should have pulled her further astern
last night. She should not have been aground at all, for
we would have to start the moment it was light, and would
need every minute of tide.

To work, then. Pull on clothes; stow bedding; scoop the
snow off the decks; and clear the ice-bound ropes round
blocks and cleats in the stinging cold, while Kirk makes
the Primus roar within a few feet of three tons of high
explosive! I don't think we are in the least frightened
that he might upset it—only intensely anxious that we
don't make fools of ourselves!

Bacon and coffee—the flat boxes make a good table.

The Customs cleared us yesterday. We have only to ask Naval Control to signal A.C.O.S. at Lyness, so that the gate in the Switha boom will be opened.

8.30. Daylight is coming. A grey day, with a freshening, bitter breeze.

9.0. At last, the water covers the engine intake. The engine starts without trouble, and runs steadily. But *Mermaid* is still on the ground. The tyre, pressed flat between the ship and the wall, begins to spring, as the breath of the sea moves into the harbour and sighs along the wall and lifts her.

9.15. Two hours of tide gone already. She slides off at last. Margaret and Kirk throw the ends of the warps on deck and swing aboard by the shrouds. I push in the gear lever, open throttle, the shaft growls and shudders, the wake foams against the wall, and slowly we swing round right-handed towards the harbour entrance.

"Good luck!" It is Captain Shearer, gazing after us rather fixedly from the end of the quay.

Breaking contact with the shore generally means breaking contact with a lot of worries. But this trip was not going according to plan. We had lost more than two hours of the tide. The wind was freshening, and it was right in our teeth. We could not lay for the edge of Dunnet, but had to pay off more than three points to fill the sails. The tide would be running faster out in the Firth than it ran in the bay, so we turned to the left and headed for Tor Ness, so as to get it under us as soon as possible.

The ship might have carried more sail; but I could not tell whether the wind would increase, and, with half the ship's ballast out and her centre of gravity raised an unknown distance, I wanted everything well under control.

All the same, as we drew out from the friendly lee of the land, I became aware that I really had painfully little idea of what would happen to us. Late as we were in getting away, I thought at first we might just make Switha Island before the reverse current began to run westwards along the South Walls of Hoy—an hour and a half before the flood stopped in the middle of the Firth. The first hour's travelling would show.

The cargo must have weighed more than the ballast we had taken out, for the ship seemed lower in the water. She was a little slower in the roll, but did not seem unduly tender. The fresh wind on her shortened sail set her just to her covering-board, so that the black water slopped in now and then amongst the petrol drums lashed on the side deck. The extra weight below decks made her carry her way over the old swell and through the jagged new run thrown up by the wind. With the wind dead ahead, it always paid to go off course in order to fill the sails, even with the engine running. They steadied the ship; and sails and engine helped each other and reduced the stopping effect of head seas.

For half-an-hour we plunged along fairly well. But as we drew out into the Firth, beyond the lee of Dunnet, the wind and the head sea, with the last of the tide against it, began to check the ship badly. She was bumping a good deal, and sprays began to blow aft and rattle over the helmsman. The weather was deteriorating. The sky was grey and thick. Presently, a flurry of snow came, and hid everything.

At that moment, the engine checked and choked. Violent manipulation of the throttle only induced it to pick up at half speed.

Marine engines were relatively new to me at this time. I had had close experience only of this one, and only during the voyage north. It had worked fairly well—well enough to allow me to refrain from doing anything to it beyond cleaning the plugs and seeing that there was enough oil in the sump. It was a pretty ancient machine, built up of various parts, some of Kelvin manufacture, some not. Later, we were to find that we could always make it go, given sufficient time to nurse it properly; and it did go for us, for hundreds and hundreds of hours, until we came to know it as we knew the sails; but it was never quite so trust-worthy!

Now, I gave up the helm to Kirk, and crouched in the doorway to study it.

The plugs were all firing, but the engine choked inter-mittently, and was not developing its power. I stopped it, and took out the float of the carburettor. The bottom of the chamber was covered with globules of rusty water. I took the jets out and blew through them, put everything back, and started the engine again.

It went off sweetly, at full bore, but in a few minutes was back at the same old game. I investigated again, and there was more water. The petrol feed pipe, which was led in a deep loop below the engine from the tank in the cockpit, must have water in it.

I undid this pipe from the carburettor and held it down into the bilge, to let the pressure from the tank push the water out of it. But barely a trickle came out of the pipe. I sucked it and spat, sucked and spat again, my mouth filling with the warm, sickly taste of petrol, while I fended my head off the hot exhaust manifold as the ship pitched and banged.

My stomach was beginning to revolt, but the lead in my heart must have kept it down. For I knew that I could never clear that pipe in time. Not only the pipe, but the tank as well, for that must be the source of the sludge—that rusty, watery mess, which accumulated in the feed system of every engine that used Pool petrol.

I stood up in the hatch, sweating and sick, to see where we were.

The snow was still thick round the ship, and visibility was practically nil. Kirk, at the helm, said he had got bearings of Dunnet and Tor Ness before it closed down. We were in the middle of the Firth, about three miles north of Dunnet. I tried to make myself believe that this snow was only a flurry, which would clear presently: that there was some chance of our finishing the journey. But I knew very well there was not. There was barely two hours of tide left. The west-going stream on the far side would begin long before we could get there.

Kirk and Margaret must have been feeling as I did; but it was up to me to make the decision. I looked past them, as if the blanket of snow beyond them would open and show me some way out; and, bless them!—they never said a word. I did not consciously go over it all again. The process of registering and plotting had been going on in my head for the past twenty-four hours. But all my desire rose up and tried to stare down the facts, like the desperate wilfulness of a child. It was no use. I had made two mistakes—being late in starting, and allowing a choked feed-pipe—and now I must crawl home rather than uselessly risk all our lives. There was but a faint consolation in the kindness of Kirk's tone—and a faint amusement in its relief—as he said solemnly: "Tony, I think you're very wise!"

We put about and paid off the sheets; and sat silent and miserable in the sudden quiet of the following wind and sea.

It took a long time to work in again out of the tide. Margaret handed round hot soup from our big flask. At half-past two, we crept in between the pier heads under the silent gaze of a little group of fishermen, and sailed the ship into her berth.

I had to go up at once and report to Naval Control. I felt that they looked at me curiously; and, as I went out, the duty officer's voice sounded quiet and expressionless behind me, saying into the telephone: "They got as far as Dunnet."

During the rest of that dreadful afternoon we took the feed system of the engine down to its last piece. We could not waste a drop of our petrol, so every pot and pan in the ship was pressed into the business of draining off the tank. Saucepans and enamel basins stood about the cockpit in the snow, full of yellow spirit, and later were carefully emptied back again, minus the red layer which had col-

lected in the bottom. By dark, we had made a job of it, and
had given the engine a full-power run, which stretched the
stern warps as hard as bars.

That evening, Kirk rebelled and insisted that we should
go and eat at the Marine, the little inn on the north quay
run by the Widow Mackay.

I remember that we slunk through the bar, which was
full of light and smoke and the laughter of trawlermen,
and that we found a queer peace in the little stiff room
beyond it, where there was shiny linoleum on the floor,
anti-macassars on the chairs, and no one to gaze curiously
at us save the Mackay family, from a photograph on the
mantelpiece, and the pair of conventional lovers in a
picture entitled "The Honeymoon", who were obviously
in no very critical frame of mind.

There, we could turn, in brief oblivion, to fried eggs and
tea, and even, as they might be ambrosia, to buns of the
incredible hygienic dryness which was then a peculiarity
of Scotch baking.

From this glimpse of heaven, we were drawn back in
time to the clean bitter night, the quay, with the pigs of
our discarded ballast poking black snouts through the
snow, the dank interior of *Mermaid*, and the too-imminent
morning.

Next day, we crossed the Firth without any trouble.

There was no snow. The engine turned over with a clean
punch and tick. The ship was pointed at Tor Ness, and
progressed crabwise until close under the South Walls of
Hoy, when she was put upon the port tack and sailed eastwards in the lee of the land to the point of Swaitha Island.
A brief check with the examination trawler, then through
the gate between the boomships, and on towards the far
hill, dim in the gathering twilight, under which was
Lyness.

To left and right lay long whalebacks of islands, bare of
everything but grass and heather, all white now with snow.

The wide sound up which we were running was merely a channel between islands. The main part of the Flow lay to the east, hidden by the ridge of Flotta.

So this was Lyness—a few huts strung along the shore, some corrugated iron sheds behind a stone quay, some oil-tanks on the hillside, and a dilapidated wooden pier, with two or three drifters tied up in a tier at the end of it. Apart from these, the great sweeps of water and whitened moor lay still and empty in the gloom.

Someone in a naval cap and a duffel coat hailed from the pier.

"What ship?"

"*Mermaid.*" For the first time there was no need to add "Southampton to Scapa Flow".

"You're Mr Bridges? Jervis is my name—agent for Baldry and Hutchinson."

The tall man in the deerstalker cap looked down at the *Mermaid* from the deck of the wooden pier. As he looked he muttered something which sounded very like an oath. Then he turned to me again.

"What have you got?" he asked.

"A hundred and twenty boxes—three tons."

"Three tons!" he repeated, and added, half to himself, "That's no bloody good to me! Did you bring any detonators?"

"Detonators! No," I said. "I've heard nothing about detonators."

"Damn and blast it all . . ." he began. Then he suddenly burst out laughing.

"Well, well," he said. "*Where* did you come from? Southampton? In *that* thing? God stiffen the Dutch! Look, my chaps will get that stuff out now. You come up with me to my office—I should like to hear more about this."

The idea of anyone but *Mermaid*'s crew doing the un-loading—or even setting foot aboard unbidden—was not at that time to be thought of. I was determined to keep our skeletons in our own cupboard, and told Jervis I would prefer to wait until the boxes were out. His long face almost flickered into a smile.

"All right," he said. "Would you mind a lift in the lorry? Come up, then, as soon as you can."

I could see that our outfit had shaken Jervis badly.

When the explosive had been unloaded I had to go and talk to him. After half-an-hour I came away from his office feeling that the situation was not entirely desperate, for he had given me a list of oddments to buy and bring over for him next trip, but that we should have to make good and go on making good, if we were to last.

At A.C.O.S. headquarters there was a shrewd inspection and summing up. We were taken there as we stood. I was not used to being interviewed by senior officers whilst dressed in fearnoughts and an oily canvas blouse, and thanked God that Margaret for once had decided to put some boots on. Kirk, as usual, looked gravely respectable. We were given typed passes, and then we hurried off to ask for the Gate.

At the point of Switha, we found we had timed it nicely. The ebb stream, which begins to run there more than two hours before the tide changes in the middle of the Firth, was just beginning to creep westwards. We crept with it no more than a cable from the shore, turning out a little for the ledge off Brims, then back close again until we were within two miles of Tor Ness. Only then did we let draw and pay off southwards for Scrabster.

As we drew out from the land, the seas suddenly humped themselves out of nothing, like a host in ambush. *Mermaid* reared and plunged; her screw, kicked out of the water by her lack of ballast, growled intermittently; and her broad behind banged down into the reverse slope like a stout old lady dropping into a chair. We held on, wondering anxiously what was going to develop. But the bad patch only lasted until we had worked out of the ebb stream. In the middle there was just an ordinary run of waves caused by the breeze; but they were steepening all the way across as the ebb began.

The sun set when we were half-way over. It lay blazing for a moment on the horizon beneath a snow cloud of furious copper, shaped like an eagle, that rushed and thickened upon us, until the air was full of snow and the copper had changed to an inky purple that blotted out everything.

In this night there grew gradually a circle of palest green. The snow thinned and stopped, the green halo cleared, and in its very centre there stood the black pillar of the Old Man of Hoy, solitary and separate from its cliff, like an appearance of the Grail.

We hastened on in the growing dark towards the shadow under the bluff, the little gap in the stone harbour walls, and the quiet place beyond, which already for us had begun to take on the kindly features of home.

It was after breakfast next morning, when we were still wallowing a little on the crest of our first small tenuous success, that Kirk brought us the telegram.

The post office had been shut when we got in the previous evening, and now, while I smoked a pipe in the cockpit and warmed my stomach in the sun, Kirk had strolled up the quay to fetch our mail.

There was a message from Harrison to say that he had sent us three cases of detonators for Lyness. And there was a telegram for Kirk, informing him of the death of a near relation and requiring his immediate presence in London.

He made no bones about it, but said that the circumstances might mean that he could not come back.

We saw him off at Thurso on the afternoon train for the south. Then, feeling like orphans, we went into the town and ordered certain rolls of felt and bags of nails for Jervis from a general store, the window of which was decorated with scythe blades, fishing lines, and teapots fashioned and painted to look like the trunks of trees.

On the way back we did not talk much, for we were

thinking of Kirk. To Margaret and me he had been like a father, and we had taken him too much for granted. It was not good to think that in our company he must sometimes have been rather alone. He had smoothed our path ashore. Such comfort as we had we owed to him. He had cooked every meal we had eaten, so far. He had been very quiet in bad moments and very patient in good ones.

Now that he was gone, the little incidents came back— how we had chaffed him about his overcoat, how the boom had nearly "knocked him out" off Skokholm, the Christmas dinner he had made at Ardrishaig, and a certain heated argument I had had with him at Inverness about the outlet for the rotary pump. "Good heavens, man," I had cried at last, "don't you know the *elements* of hydrostatics?" I wondered now how I could have said such an appalling thing to anyone!

8

THE SECOND RUN

"Which inlet or gulf this afternoon, and in the night,
we passed over: where to our great admiration we saw the
sea falling down into the gulf with a mighty overfal, and
roring, and with divers circular motions like whirlpooles,
in such sort as forcible streams pass thorow the arches of
bridges."
—John Davis: Log Note for 31st July 1587, Third
Voyage for the Discovery of the North-West Passage

WE WERE not given much time to sorrow over
Kirk's departure. The day after he left, it began
to blow.

It was a wind out of the east, that grew gradually through
the day, with a high, steady glass, and a dull sky, until by
nightfall it was a gale. And it stayed like that, all that night
and through the next day, and the next, and the next. For
eleven days the wind blew, never varying in direction
beyond east to south-east, never dropping below thirty
miles an hour, rising at times to eighty.

It covered the Firth with a grey blanket of broken seas;
it howled with a savage insistence through the day, through
the night, filling the rocking cabin of the *Mermaid* with
its wet, mournful weird, and with an endless droning and
tapping of the rigging on the mast, which we could not
still, no matter how we lashed it. The days passed in a black
haze, through which in all that time the sun never shone
even for a single moment. It was as though the Earth had
stopped turning, as it did in H. G. Wells's story of the
Man who could work Miracles, and this wind was the
break-up of creation.

So long as we lived, however, it was quite plain that we were to be allotted a job—life and work, as we were beginning to realise, being synonymous. Our daily, almost hourly, work consisted in keeping the ship in one piece in the run that was coming into the harbour.

This run was not the long heave that came in during westerly gales: it was a much shorter and more active disturbance, caused by the seas running straight in at the harbour mouth. Thurso Bay, from Dunnet to Scrabster Harbour, was four miles across, a distance quite sufficient for the east gale to raise a short sea, which burst continually against the outer quay and charged through the narrow entrance between the end of that quay and the *St Ninian's* berth. This upheaval spread itself over the little harbour, and kept all small craft lifting and falling, and charging incessantly to and fro against their warps.

The east wind had another effect, which we did not fully appreciate until the second night.

After a day spent in parcelling and adjusting warps and fenders, we had decided that the west wall was untenable; and before dark, in the course of two hours' slow, heavy work, had shifted the boat to a berth on the south quay, ahead of the tiers of the Wick seine-net boats. (The R.N. store ship, the *Benduff*, which normally used that berth, was fortunately away in Orkney.)

Here we had hoped that she would remain afloat at low water. But we were soon disillusioned. The east wind, blowing behind the ebb tide, reduced the height of water by over a foot. A solid crash as her heel took the ground sent us flying on deck. The wind on her tall mast was holding her off the wall, and we had just time, with great effort, to shorten the warps until she lay in close enough to list against it at the proper angle before she took the ground. This she did with a series of heartbreaking bumps which lasted half-an-hour, before the water had gone sufficiently to lift her no more.

The bottom was of sand, but, even so, the punishment

she took made me wonder how much longer she could stand it. There was no better berth, even had there been no other ships, for, as the tide ran on towards springs, the harbour dried completely. Where we were lying, we at least had all the shelter there was. But as the after part of the keel struck and struck again, it became obvious that something must be done.

The crisis came on the second night, when, just before she settled down, the ship struck with a shock that put out the cabin lamp.

As soon as the tide came again, we took a coil of seizing wire and some tools and a torch, and went on deck.

Amongst our motley collection of fenders were two large lorry tyres, each weighing about eighty pounds. Working in the masked glow of the torch, we lashed the two tyres together, one on top of the other, and fastened a three-fathom length of coir warp to each side of the bundle. When the ship floated, we passed one of these lines under her stern with the boathook, dropped the lashed tyres over the side, and, after much prodding with the boathook in the heaving water, got them adjusted underneath her keel, and the lines made fast on either side of the ship. By the time we could do no more, the tide was near the flood, the *Mermaid*'s deck stood above the quay, and sprays from the seas outside were flying over us. At last, ragged with strain and effort, we went below and made some soup, and turned in about midnight.

Soon after six next morning I was awakened by the familiar jar and shudder, and turned out to watch the ship down. The wind was screaming as hard as ever, the ship rising and falling as before, but the impact was noticeably softer; our improvised shock absorber seemed to be doing its job. During the succeeding days we had to adjust it at every tide, and expended much rope in replacing the chafed lines.

We had no means of recording from day to day the exact force of the wind, and the general maximum and minimum for those eleven days were given to us from A.C.O.S. only after we had crossed again to Orkney. It never for one moment sank below the status of a half-gale, but I believe that it was at its worst during the first week, and that, although towards the end it rose at times to its full fury, it was, in fact, during the last three or four days, gradually petering out.

We could not leave the ship, except for an hour or two either side of the time of high water. Then, using our combined forces to drag one end of her in to the quay, we jumped ashore and did what jobs we had to do, such as shopping, fetching fresh water, and so on.

Sometimes, to relieve the strain and tedium, we went for a stamp along the brae, head down, with staggering steps; watching the whitened sea; revisiting often a place where a little freshwater runnel was whipped back continually from the cliff edge by the rising blast, so that the icicles round it pointed upwards as well as down; and, now and then, to cheer and warm ourselves, running full tilt down steep slopes with giant strides, borne up by the living gale.

The detonators arrived on the fifth day. The news of their arrival coincided with a telegram from Jervis asking rather briefly when he might expect them.

The gale was just supportable, without this extra worry. How, I thought, could we load detonators and risk staying loaded, possibly for days, with the ship trying to bang her keel through her kelson at every ebb? Yet load we must, because at any time the gale might blow itself out, or slack away just enough to give us the chance that we must not miss.

On the morning of the seventh day there was a sufficient lull to let us motor across the harbour to the five-hundred-weight crane on the east quay. I hired a lorry to bring down Jervis's nails and roofing-felt, and the detonators—three red-painted steel cases, each two feet square and weighing a couple of hundredweight. I had their measurements beforehand, and we had removed the cabin door to get them in, since they were too big for the skylight. The loading went satisfactorily, and we trundled back to our berth, to watch and wait.

Each morning, when the *St Ola* was about to sail, I would stagger round to the east quay and ask Captain Swanson what he thought of it. Each morning he was equally pessimistic. Indeed, he must have thought us a pair of young people who required their heads seen to.

Captain Swanson was the Grand Old Man of the Pentland Firth; he had crossed it twice a day nearly every day for fifty years. At seventy-five he was still crossing it, though now he had a chair placed in the wheelhouse to relieve occasionally the strain of eight hours' standing. Weather stopped him, on the average, four days in the year. In practice, that meant that he would cross in any wind of less than eighty or ninety miles an hour; and I have watched him take the 500-ton *St Ola* out when she was showing her keel over the seas as soon as she cleared the entrance.

He was a big man, with white hair and beard, pink cheeks, and blue eyes that were very shrewd, clear, and kind. I would hover in his vicinity while he had a last word with the assistant harbourmaster, both streaming with the spray that dashed over the end of the pier. When he noticed me and heard my petition, he shook his head. "Tcha, never think of it!" he said. "Your sails would be blown out o' the bolt ropes. Yon boatie wad never cross, the day!" I suspected that part of his meaning was not to have our blood upon his conscience; but, after looking and frowning awhile into the quivering tunnels of the wind, I was forced to agree with him.

On the ninth day came a second telegram from Jervis. "Hurry along," it said, "with those detonators."

Jervis wanted those detonators, wanted them very badly indeed. I cursed Cooke and Harrison with the desperation of impotence. They had told me nothing whatsoever about detonators. What I had undertaken to deliver, once fortnightly, was five tons of gelignite. To be stuck with detonators was clean outside my contract. Yet Jervis wanted them; and upon our ability to deliver them, over and above bags of nails, rolls of roofing felt, and anything else that might be required, seemed to depend the continuance of our existence in the neighbourhood.

I weakened to the extent of going up to Thurso and asking the agent there for the North of Scotland Company whether the *St Ola* or the *St Ninian* would take them, just for this time—and received, as I had expected, a flat no.

The cases, which occupied most of the floor space in *Mermaid*'s cabin, now served as a dining-table. When we had eaten our soup and bread and cheese, Margaret and I spread out on them the large chart of the Firth and the little inset which gave twelve-hourly pictures of the tide, and settled down to find out whether we could cross.

High water, by this time, had come round to about three o'clock—high water, that is to say, in the middle of the Firth. We would need at least three hours of the flood tide to make our easting. But the wind was flat against it— wind against tide: the conflict that, so far, we believed we could not face.

We turned again to the general picture of the Firth: to the analogy of the Atlantic and the North Sea as two pools in a river, and of the Firth as the "run" or "stickle" connecting them, and the two islands of Stroma and Swona as rocks in the neck between the two pools. Where you have water travelling as fast as it did in the Firth, thinking of it as a river gives a better idea than thinking of it as sea; and, as a fisherman, I felt happier thinking of it like that.

When the water in a river flows from one pool to another through a narrow neck, it breaks only after it has passed through the neck and begins to spread out. The water in the tail of the upper pool and in the neck itself flows smoothly.

The marks for the overfalls on the chart confirmed that

the same thing applied to the Firth. When the tide was ebbing—that is to say, flowing to the west—the broken water of the stickle formed on the Atlantic side. When the tide was flooding—flowing to the east—the stickle would form in the North Sea.

When the tide was flooding, the western end of the Firth would be smooth, like the "glide" at the tail of the upper pool where the water begins to gather speed, before it flows through the neck, piles up round the rocks, and breaks as it emerges into the lower one. In this east wind, when the tide was flooding, the real mess would be off the Pentland Skerries and in the Bores of Duncansby, east of Stroma and Swona, in the North Sea.

If our analogy was correct, it did not seem likely that in these conditions the wind, hard as it was, would disturb very seriously the naturally unbroken "glide" of the flood tide west of the two islands. It would chop and whiten it, but the sea walls would not form until the outpouring waters met, between the two islands, the drift from the North Sea. The islands themselves would break much of this incoming drift, as also would the point of St Johns.

Strategically, then, we could probably say that there would be no seas of the sheerly impossible kind between us and our goal. The doubtful places would be the open gap, four miles across, between the islands, and the last four miles between Swona and the Switha entrance. In the open gap, which we must cross at slack water, so as not to be carried through, the wind and its attendant beam sea might be too much for the boat. In the last four miles, between Swona and Switha, the wind, combined with the ebb stream, which would have been running there for at least two hours before the tide stood still in the middle of the Firth, might set us westwards beyond the Switha entrance before we could get across.

The time of tide was right. High water in the middle would be at about two p.m. If we were near Swona at that time, we should get in before dark.

The third strategic factor was the actual force of the wind. It must not be too great to allow a close-reefed mainsail; for if we struck any badly disturbed water the engine would be useless.

Granted all these overriding necessities, the tactical situation appeared to be fairly simple. The key of the thing was to time the journey so as to cross the gap between the islands at slack water. The first four miles would be shielded by Dunnet Head. From there to St Johns we should probably find reasonably quiet water close inshore. At St Johns we could pay off and get into the lee of Stroma. After that, we must hope to find conditions in the gap not too severe: if the sea there was plain, it could be quite large without being dangerous. Then we should find another lee behind Swona. Lastly, there was the four-mile rush, to be taken crabwise, across the ebb stream to the point of Switha; we thought the boat, with the wind on her quarter, would travel fast enough to give us command of the fierce set we should find there.

Finally, there was, for once, a reasonable chance of retreat. I did not think we should need it, since the probability was that we should either be drowned or get through, but in some such event as snow, or physical injury to the ship or to one of the crew, it would be possible, at the change of tide, with the wind and tide together, to turn round and run back home.

Looked at as closely as this, the thing did seem manageable. We could not, of course, look at it as closely as we should be looking at it from *Mermaid*'s deck; but we had to spirit ourselves as nearly as we could into that situation.

We went out and considered the wind. It was certainly blowing pretty hard. One circumstance would increase our chances very much. If the wind would shift even to southeast, it would fill the sails as far as the point of St Johns, and then, if we kept really close to the islands, we should have it on our quarter to push us across the fierce ebb stream we should have to encounter in the last four miles.

The barometer, high and rock steady, gave no clue. But as we stood on the quay, questing into the blast, trying to sense the dumb message that it hammered upon our eyelids, there did seem to be a change, a veering of pressure, ever so slight, in those endless torrents of air, towards the south.

We started out next morning, with three reefs down, close-hauled on the starboard tack, heading for the point of Dunnet. The three cases of detonators were well chocked off with the rolls of felt and the amorphous sacks of nails, and the total of cargo made a fine addition to our ballast.

The wind howled as wetly as ever; but there was a distinct relief in being out dealing with it, after so long watching and being sickened by it: waiting defensively for what it would do next.

The sea, this side of Dunnet, was merely a heavy chop. The engine ran rather clamorously. The spray mingled with the sleet in the wind. The ship, her lee deck awash, pressed on steadily, not yet helped much by the flood tide, which ran slackly in the hollow of the bay.

We felt extraordinarily cheerful. Whether it was the release into activity after days of strain, or the idea that because we had done the trip once it had become a familiar road, or just that at last the job had become worth while—whatever the cause, we were as light-hearted as though we were starting on an ocean race.

"Jean-ne Fiet-te (*we sang*)
    Profitez du temps!
  La violet-te
    Se cueille au printemps!"

Nobody could hear us, so it did not matter!

We had lunch, and Dunnet came abeam more or less on time. For a while we were practically becalmed beneath the cliff; then we came into the full sweep of the tide, and were carried quickly round the corner and into a sea which was disturbed where the wind again met it in full blast.

For some time the ship was thrown about heavily, and the engine choked and stopped.

Before going to start it, I found that the cone clutch had jammed in the "ahead" position. It was the first time this had happened, and I could not free it for fear of breaking the lever. (Later, we kept a wooden wedge and a four-pound hammer in the cockpit for this particular emergency.)

The engine started again, in gear, but it was as sick as it had been during the abortive first run—and for the same reason: a choked feed system. Apparently, the feed would have to be cleared as a matter of routine maintenance after every journey. Just now, I could do nothing with it; and we could not turn back until the tide slackened. However, the engine had done its job, in helping to push us across the slack water of Thurso Bay. Now, both tide and wind were in our favour, and from this point onwards the wind was such as to render the engine a work of supererogation.

When we reached St Johns we turned slightly left, and could free the sheets to shoot across the inner sound for the lee of Stroma. We had traversed this ground three weeks earlier, on the way to Scrabster. On that day the sea had been asleep in a grey haze. Now it was awake and menacing, and the peaceful haze had become a driven mass of water and air. We could not see Stroma, although only two miles away from it when we paid off; there was only a desolation of white seas disappearing into the void.

There was a great weight in the wind. The main sheets, paid far off, were stretched as hard as bars to the end of the boom, far outside the clew of the treble-reefed mainsail. But, although so comprehensive, it was a reliable kind of wind. There were no squalls, no shifts, no great guns in it. It blew hard and steady, just as it had been blowing for the past ten days, and as it might apparently blow for ever—a black emanation of power, as though some pagan king, brooding in the uttermost steppes, had loosed his hosts upon the world.

We had to set a compass course for Stroma. Very soon we came up to it—a dim outline close aboard to starboard, setting a bound to the circumambient white.

The sea here was quiet. Too quiet, in fact, for presently we ran into a vast patch where it was oily smooth, where even the gale did not ruffle its surface, spreading and squirming as though it were about to boil; and we realised that the great eddy had begun to form, and that therefore the tide had begun to ebb.

With the wind well on the quarter now, the ship raced on over a nightmare ballroom floor, and suddenly, in the murk ahead, there stood up a low rim of sea, quite stationary, breaking steadily. There was no way round it, and we took it with a heave and a plunge, and at once found ourselves pitching every way in the newly forming race on the outer edge of the eddy.

We were, as we knew, in the worst spot in the Firth, the place called the Swelkie, where, on the ebb tide in any breath of westerly wind, the sea resolves itself into precipices which stand and break upon themselves until the tide ends. In this east wind it was harmless. But we were glad to win clear of the crazy waters into the large wholesome beam sea which was sweeping regular and clean through the gap.

As we had suspected, this beam sea set us severely to the west. We clawed up at forty-five degrees, travelling furiously over the waves, but very slowly over the ground, towards the lee of Swona.

I think that was the most exciting four miles I have ever done in a sailing boat. The seas were enormous, and the boat was travelling at top speed. Two things made it possible—the quartering wind and the beginning of the ebb tide, which ran with the wind and prevented the seas from breaking seriously. *Mermaid* was literally hurled along, without much pitch or roll, slung all her length up to the crests and dropped into the hollows. Only now and then, as she rose, would a partly breaking top crash against the full length of her bilge and send sheets of spray as high as the gaff jaws.

After what seemed a long time we reached Swona, and, once in its eddy, worked up almost to the rocks, so as to gain every inch of ground before making the final dash across the channel to Switha, where the ebb was now running like a millrace.

But for the strength of the wind, the tide there would have beaten us. I don't know at what speed the stream was running. The tides were still very close to springs, and when we were half-way across and raised the loom of the steep south side of Switha the white along its base seemed to be moving visibly westwards. The *Mermaid* was probably travelling at near her maximum speed, and, on a steep slant, with all the drive that the wind could give her, she slowly made good the crossing.

For a time it was doubtful whether she would do it. If she missed Switha we were done for, and would have to try and go back.

Gradually she worked in, gaining slowly the weather gauge after she had won past the middle of the channel; but in order to clear the point of the island she had to be pointed almost due east, so that she finally scraped past the end of it close-hauled. The examination vessel did not hold us up: she came plunging up within speaking distance, spray flying over her, and waved to us to go on.

And so, for the second time, we entered the sanctuary and ran, pursued by considerable but harmless seas, towards the boom. An ex-seine-net fishing vessel, which was patrolling the boom, met us on the other side and insisted on giving us a tow to Lyness; but the tow-rope sagged between the two vessels as we drove up on him faster than his engines could push him out of our way.

The wind had risen again, in what proved to be its final burst of fury, and, long before we reached Lyness, the flying dusk was swallowed up in a screaming blackness of night.

9

FIRE

"To all these that column of smoke did in a manner
address itself. 'Look here!' it said, 'this, within limits, is
your affair. What are you going to do?'"

H. G. WELLS: *The History of Mr Polly*

SLEEP IS a state of life in which we have to spend a
good deal of time, and it is one of the most precious
parts of it.

One should be a connoisseur of sleep, as of food, or wine,
or water, or of what one does. As death should be the
crown of life, so should sleep be the crown of days; and, as
the day has been spent, so will be the quality of the sleep
that follows.

If I am right, our performances of the previous day could
not have been so unnatural as perhaps they sound, for I
remember that night as one of the forty-fathom nights,
when we drank sleep as though it were a frosted wine.

We were jerked back into the world by a heavy bump
alongside and the growl of a reversed propeller.

A voice hailing, and the sound of feet on deck, completed the circuit which wrenched us agonisingly out of
our bunks to pull on trousers and ganseys and boots. We
put our heads out, to find Baldry's launch alongside, with
Jervis and two others in her cockpit, and his lame boatman,
Jerry, making fast her lines. They wore oilskins, for it was
still blowing and the dawn was bitter with sleet.

I was uncertain of our reception, for we had been late,
as usual, and this call, so early in the day, might be in the
nature of a visitation. I began by shouting a nervous
apology across the rocking gunwales.

"Have you got any detonators for us?"

"Yes—three cases. And the felt and the nails."

Jervis knew we had them, but he scrambled across, to peer into our cabin, and see for himself. Then he turned and grinned, as though one more layer of incredulity had been dissolved.

"I'm glad to see you!" he said, making his face a tragicomedy of relief, and shaking my hand. "I never expected you to come in this weather. When I got your wire, yesterday morning, I felt like a murderer!"

I said that I thought the wording of his last telegram had been most moderate!

"Well, I didn't want you to commit suicide. But what could I do? We've been raising heaven and earth to get detonators. The Navy hadn't got any. Nobody had any. No one except you showed any signs of bringing any. We're using the last of our stock now, and if you hadn't appeared there would have been five hundred men idle by midday. For the past week I've been dreaming of detonators until I felt like shoving one of the blasted things . . . !"

All this sounded delightful, but I had to explain that we were engineless until we could do some repairs. At this Jerry brought some tools and freed the clutch for us in a moment. Then they relieved us of the felt and nails, and said a lorry would be at the wooden pier for the detonators in a couple of hours' time.

The breakfast which Margaret proceeded to make was really the high point of the expedition.

Food, like sleep, is one of the major mercies; and food made over Primuses and eaten fresh and hot from Woolworth plates and mugs on one of Messrs Nobel's detonator cases in the cabin of a small cutter after a successful voyage is food with a difference. We ate our porridge and bacon and eggs, and kept the coffee hot, and made toast on an asbestos mat over the Primus, as we had done now for the

past three months; but this morning we did it with the
abandon of a couple of infants at a picnic.

It was almost with a sense of injury that we turned to
washing up, and then to the business of starting the engine
and taking the *Mermaid* alongside the wooden pier. We
found that the engine would work if one of us kept a finger
on the float of the carburettor: this served, until we were
alongside.

At Scrabster we found that a further load of gelignite
had arrived.

This was a short load of two and a half tons—100 boxes
—which we had asked for, seeing that there were still two
tons—80 boxes—left over from the first consignment.
The railway was agitating for the release of the gunpowder
vans. We debated whether we could take the lot in one
journey. A single run had not been enough to show what
Mermaid's working capacity really was. Three tons had
been easy. Five was mathematically possible. Four tons
seemed to be about the mark, allowing a reasonable margin
for comfort and safety. We proposed now to take four-and-
a-half. The glass remained high and the weather, after the
long gale, had entered a period of utter calm, that looked
as though it might last at least a day or two; so we decided
to try.

By this time, I had made arrangements with a private
haulier who had a couple of lorries, to bring our stuff down
from the station.

The stack of 180 boxes looked enormous on the quay.
This time, we could not load until late at night, when the
flood tide had brought the *Mermaid*'s deck level with the
top of the wall; since, with only two of us, we could not
use the gaff and sling, and would have to hand the stuff
first on to the deck and then from the deck through the
skylight into the cabin. Had we waited a day we could have
got help, but I was anxious to catch the flood tide for a
crossing next morning.

Margaret and I began loading at nine p.m. in a clear starlight, reddened by the shifting curtains of a brilliant aurora.

At ten, the fishermen began coming down the quay from Mother Mackay's inn.

We were still a curiosity to them, and a few came and watched us for a while, and we had to refuse several kindly-meant but rather bibulous offers of help. They went on to their boats, all except one, a certain Skipper McMaster, whom we had met soon after we arrived. He was a long pirate of a man—a muzzy giant, with the black set of brow that betokens a berserk temper, and the fineness of jaw and eye that keeps it mostly under control. It was a striking, salacious face, a face that would have been magnificent if it had not been so perpetually burdened with the support of liquor. This made it glow like a stove, and gave it a humorous, quizzical expression, as though its owner had just been the indulgent victim of some practical joke. McMaster was a Wick man, and he owned a filthy boat called *Daffodil*, crewed by a collection of attractive troglodytes.

This character now looked down unsteadily from the edge of the quay and enquired hoarsely: "Are ye bedded?" Then seeing us, he added sadly "Why are ye no bedded?"

He then sat down amongst the boxes and commenced a somewhat incoherent conversation with us.

"Mam," he said, addressing Margaret, "ye'll forgive my askin'—I've had a wee drink or two, ye know, and I'm no juist masel' the night—eh, forgie me—but, are ye an Admiral's daughter?"

Margaret disclaimed the honour, and he muttered—with relief, I thought, and without the slightest intention to offend: "Oh, I see, I see—just common people."

He then offered repeatedly to help us, and our gentle but persistent refusal intrigued his obstinacy.

Presently he lit a cigarette. I told him that when gelignite freezes it becomes highly unstable and is apt to go off at a touch. This moved him not at all. We stopped talking and went on with our job, sweating with the work, and keeping a covert eye on his cigarette. He smoked it to the end, ground it out on the top of a box, and lit another.

I think it was the cold, more than our grim silence, which at last drove him away.

"Mind the froshty ones!" he said at last, flicking ash amongst the boxes and getting unsteadily to his feet. "I say —mind the froshty ones! Goo' night!"

We finished up at about two a.m., dead beat.

The cabin was full to the coamings. The stack overflowed aft from the inner door and filled both quarter berths, leaving barely room to get at the starting handle of the engine. If it blows now, I thought, and she starts bumping, God help us.

But the glass had not moved, and the night was utterly still. Only the folds of red and green flickered in the sky, as though stirred by some ghostly draught, and seemed to rustle as they moved. We watched for a time, but were too weary to stay long on deck. Margaret disappeared into the fo'c'sle, and I spread a mattress and some blankets on the level roof of boxes in the cabin, crawled into the eighteen inches of space under the skylight, and fell into an outrage of sleep.

The morning dawned in a clear beauty of stillness and light, as it had for the past two days. We had asked for the Gate at the naval control office the night before, and I had only to walk along and get confirmation from the duty officer before we set out.

The Firth was as flat as the Round Pond. We made breakfast and had it in the cockpit, spreading plates and cups about the cabin top and the deck. The tide was barely on the turn and we had the full six hours of the flood ahead of us. The mainsail hung limply from the gaff in gentle folds that there was not breath enough to fill.

The crossing, and the unloading next morning, were managed without any difficulty. That day, it was just possible, by starting back as soon as the unloading was finished, to re-cross on the last of the morning ebb. The spell of perfect calm continued, as though the weather were convalescing after the long gale.

Three cargoes successfully carried had begun to give the operation an air of familiarity. And they had at last made it solvent. On arrival at Scrabster the firm was £90 in debt. Kirk and Margaret and I had financed it in turn, each contributing what pounds could be scraped up from week to week. One of us had gone so far as to borrow from the bank, which indulgently provided £30 without security. Now, when the freight was paid, there would be a balance.

It has been said that to earn a pound and spend a guinea, and vice versa, is the difference between misery and happiness. There is a lot in that. One way and another, that afternoon, we felt pretty good.

No more gelignite was due at Thurso for another week. Jervis had now a fortnight's supply in hand. For the first time for three months the strain eased a little, and we looked forward to a rather quieter life for the next day or two.

There was always plenty to do. Thurso, two miles off, had to be visited frequently, generally on foot, for various errands; food had to be cooked; at every low water warps had to be tended and the ship watched safely down.

Paper work was beginning to intrude itself. At this time the office furniture consisted of one brown paper folder and one sixpenny writing-pad. There was no typewriter. Letters were drafted in pencil, and copied out twice in ink, like mediaeval manuscripts.

We suffered our first introduction to forms: forms for petrol, Customs forms, forms for rations. The full, paralysing hurricane of forms had not yet set in, but already it seemed impossible even for two people to run a fifteen-ton cutter without them. At first, we were rather proud of them. The *transire*, with its stiff green card and blob of sealing-wax, giving "authority for the departure of a ship from a port in the United Kingdom", was a royal charter to adventure, and the "Application for Permission to Load Explosives" was dangerous and select. It seemed delightful and proper to see myself described as "Master", and the *Mermaid* as a "ship" of so many tons burden!

The time for writing was the evening, when work with dirty objects of all kinds was temporarily over and our hands could, for a while, be made more or less clean. I would start in, at the little folding table, while Margaret put the finishing touches to supper.

There was no attempt at a galley in the *Mermaid*. For cooking, Margaret's mainstay consisted of two Primus stoves on a bench in the fo'c'sle. There was also the small blue-flame stove which Kirk had bought in Teignmouth. We had come to regard the Primus as one of the great inventions of all time and as being completely foolproof and safe. We used them, very wrongly, perhaps, but almost inevitably, when there were explosives on board. The blue-flame heater was an altogether different proposition, for the flame was apt to creep and smoke when not constantly watched.

There was not a great deal of room in *Mermaid*'s cabin. The floor space measured six feet long by about four feet wide at the after end. On either side, the bunks were set beneath the side decks. Forward, the coaming of the coach roof overhung the floor, which extended a foot or so under the low fo'c'sle deck before reaching the fo'c'sle partition. There was no headroom there for a hot, exposed flame. The only position in which the stove could be placed, with sufficient headroom to carry off the heat, was against the partition at the after end of the cabin. There, six feet separated it from the coach roof.

The partition was made of matchboard, covered thickly with white enamel paint. On the back of it—the quarter-berth side—were hooks covered with oilskins, spare pull-overs, blouses and caps, and some of our shore clothes. To the front of it, at the place where the stove stood, we had screwed a piece of asbestos about a foot wide and two feet high, to protect the partition from the heat. This, on and off, for three months, it had succeeded in doing.

On the second night after our last return from Orkney, I was sitting at the table writing a letter to Harrison. The lamp, in gymbals in the middle of the forward coaming, shone on white paint, now marred here and there by oily finger-marks, and filled the cabin with light. From the little open square of the fo'c'sle door, marked by a dimmer illumination, came the roar of the Primuses and a comforting smell of curry, nearing perfection. On the blue-flame stove, close beside me, stood an asbestos mat, on the top of which was a pot containing rice pudding.

A ship of about a thousand tons had come in that day —a big ship for the tiny harbour—called the *Robert Dundas*: an Army store ship. The *Benduff* being still away, we were lying in her berth on the south wall, and the *Robert Dundas* was berthed close behind us. I think it was that fact that saved the *Mermaid*'s life.

I had finished my letter, and was just getting up, when I became aware of a sudden strong smell of scorched paint. I looked first of all at the roof over the lamp. That appeared to be all right. The brass protector was in place, and only its shadow marked the paint above it.

Then I looked at the stove. That appeared to be all right, too, though the flame had crept rather high, and the heat, bottled up under the pot and the mat, was intense. I went through the opening (from which we had removed the door when we loaded the detonators) into the quarter-berth space to look at the back of the partition and see if anything was happening there. It was dark there and I could not see clearly, but I touched the paint and felt it scorching hot. The torch was in the cockpit. I hurriedly opened the door to fetch it: a cold draught rushed in, and behind me I heard a sudden "whoof", and turning, saw flame burst round the oilskins from the back of the partition.

I shut the cockpit door immediately, shouted to Margaret, and tried to smother the fire with the numerous damp garments hanging from the hooks. But the oilskins must have been dried out thoroughly by the gradually scorching partition and they were well alight.

Margaret had turned off the Primuses and pushed both them and the paraffin tin out through the fo'c'sle hatch. I had time to reach the offending heater, turn it out, and run with it into the cockpit. Margaret came after me, having collected the barometer, our "office file", a few books, and a coat or two, on her way through the cabin. Then I pulled the extinguisher from its bracket above the engine and began squirting it at the blazing partition.

The extinguisher was one of those things that produce chlorine gas. It was probably quite good at putting out fires in the wide open spaces. The only effect it had in the present circumstances was to prevent us, from that time on, from getting anywhere near the fire. I pointed it, as I had been taught, at the base of the fire: the bottom of the partition, where the fire had started. I thought that would be the only place where the fire would have had time to take hold. Dense clouds of choking fog at once filled the quarter-berth space and took me by the throat. For a few moments I knew what it feels like to be killed by chlorine gas. I could not see; I could not breathe; nor do anything, but choke and choke.

With the idea of starving the fire of air, I had been unwilling to open the cockpit door. Now Margaret opened it, and I got into the cockpit and could do nothing for a minute or two but lean on the coaming and feel as though I should choke my heart out. Margaret squirted the extinguisher into the fog until it was empty. Then she shut the door.

As the deadly constriction in my lungs eased I could see through the skylight the horrible red glow of flames working below. The glass cracked and pieces of it fell in; a smoky tongue licked up at the bulge of the tied mainsail.

The cabin must be full of fire. There was a bucket on deck, with a lanyard on it. Margaret grabbed it and began sluicing water over the sail and down the skylight.

At about this time, a voice from the quay said, conversationally: "Have you got a fire down there?"

"Yes," I croaked.

"Want any help?"

I said "Yes, please"; and it occurred to me that this sounded rather as though the enquirer had offered me a second cup of tea.

There were three or four young lads in the group on the quay—officers from the *Robert Dundas* returning to their ship after an evening ashore. Two of them jumped aboard us. The others ran to their ship for more buckets.

We opened the cockpit door, and they took it in turns to dash through and throw their bucketfuls into the void, where the fog was shot with running, flickering flames. Where we had thrown low, they threw high, up under the roof and to either side.

"Fire's running on the paint," said one. "We'll have it out in a minute. Billy, keep that sail wet."

It took them about a quarter of an hour to kill out the fire from the last nooks and corners of the roof where it had crept to feed on the coat of rich paint. The hissing continued for a while beyond the fog; then the last bucketfuls splashed into darkness; and the horror had passed.

It was some minutes before I could convince myself that the *Mermaid* still existed. Surprise, and a vast relief, grew, as it appeared that outwardly she was still exactly the same as before. The only traces of the fire that could be discovered by the light of the torch were a cracked scuttle or two, an absence of glass in the skylight, and a scorched patch immediately above it in the belly of the mainsail. Nowhere had the fire broken through the coach roof. As the First Officer of the *Dundas* had remarked, it must have run over the paint, and been quenched by the prompt help of himself and his party before it could take deep hold. If

he and his friends had not happened to be passing at the
critical moment, it might have been a quarter of an hour
before we could have found help—long enough for the fire
to have become rooted in the wood.

As we recovered ourselves, we saw another providential
aspect to the affair. Our rescuers were strangers. They
might barely have heard that our vessel was being used for
explosives; but the fact would probably not have registered sufficiently to cause them any grievous alarm. If we
had had to get help from the duty drifter, or, worse still,
from Naval Control, the balloon would very definitely be
up. True, they would know all about it tomorrow, but, by
tomorrow, if the *Mermaid* showed no external signs, the
fire would have shrunk to a minor incident. After all,
nobody had been hurt; nobody, except ourselves, had even
dirtied their clothes; and it had all been over very quickly.

These were the first considerations. The pit had yawned
and closed again, leaving us merely without a home.

It had been bare enough, that little cabin, with its board
floor, its hard bunks, and its tiny rickety table, covered with
oilcloth. But for three months we had had no other place
to live in. Each of its fittings and each of our small possessions had acquired a significance and a memory. Now, the
torchlight showed a pool of filthy water in a black cave.
Objects could be distinguished only as ghostly, furry shapes
against a matt background.

It was too late to make a mark on it that night. And we
had not the heart to try. Fire, out of control, is a shocking,
sickening disintegration, that eats and burns its beholder
as it does the illicit fuel it feeds on. We felt we needed
nothing so much as a drink.

We were in no shape to go on board the *Dundas*, but
they insisted. They started us off with half a tumbler of
Scotch, then provided hot water and soap in a real bathroom, and, when we had gone through the motions of
removing the grime, made us sit down to a supper of cold
meat.

When it came to their offering us beds, we felt we could not let them go so far.

In the frosty moonlight we walked round the quays to the Marine Hotel to throw ourselves on the mercy of Mother Mackay. Her windows shone only with the blank glitter of the moon; and the little lady's voice, when she presently threw up a window in response to our knocking, was not cordial. But she was a good soul. Wrapped in a black shawl, she fetched us in, bade us wait in the bar "while Ah see til the room", and presently led us upstairs to a large room containing two beds which had been prudently stripped of sheets and pillowcases and provided with rough blankets. We took off coats and trousers—the outermost, grimiest shell of our covering—and made fast to the very bollards of sleep.

For the next ten days we slept at the Marine, but we had not the nerve to ask for food: that would have meant sitting in the front parlour, a thing we simply could not get clean enough to do. *Mermaid*'s fo'c'sle, though black, had not been entered by the fire; the Primus stoves were intact; so we could cook food there.

The morning after the fire, we crept out early, bought a loaf and some eggs from Mrs Maclaren at the post office, and went down to our unfortunate ship.

The still, clear weather was holding. This morning, the eastern sky had the transparent glow in it, and distant sounds of that clear far-carrying quality, which herald a perfect day. The weather, in this ultimate corner of the kingdom, could be as awful as a nightmare or as beautiful as the flax of dream. This was one of the good spells, and it helped very much to carry us over the misery of the next ten days.

The whole of the inside of the *Mermaid* was covered with a thick black fur, like that which gathers in the chimney of a lamp which has been smoking for a long time. There was so much of it that we wondered what kind of weapon to attack it with. We discussed this at length over

breakfast. Then we went up to Thurso, and bought two
wire brushes, two scrubbing brushes, a four-pound bar of
yellow soap, and two dozen sheets of sandpaper. This, we
thought, would do for a start. Scrapers we already had.

There was surprisingly little serious damage. All glass
had been cracked. There was a hole in one cloth of the
mainsail, which we had enough canvas to repair. All paintwork above the level of the bunks was destroyed. The
boarding of the partition where the fire had started was
reduced to obscene fangs; but that was not a vital part of
the ship's structure. Nowhere had the fire taken deep hold.
The worst charring was in the beams of the coach roof, but
on scraping one of them we came to sound wood about a
quarter of an inch below the charcoal crust.

The losses in gear, too, were small. The garments on the
partition, of course, had disappeared, and they included
our oilskins, one or two good jerseys—old friends of many
a day—and all our shore clothes. One or two of the books in
the minute shelf on the forward coaming were wrecked:
these had been standing loosely and the flames had got
round them; but the others, including our sea-Bible, Claud
Worth's *Yacht Cruising*, were only scorched at the edges.
Paper, when tightly packed, is one of the most in-
destructible of substances. One or two blankets had gone,
and others had large holes burnt in them; but they must
early have been rendered non-inflammable by being
deluged with water. The same applied to the mattresses.
Nothing in the cupboards or in the lockers under the
bunks had been hurt in the least. Nor had our folding
table, which must have stood solitary in the midst of the
conflagration, well clear of the blazing paintwork. Except
to run along the roof, the fire had not come abaft the partition, so that the patent log and the engine, the charts, and
the mass of spare gear we carried in the quarter-berth
bunks (when not occupied by bodies or explosives) was
untouched.

Having made a rough estimate of the damage, we began

work with scrapers on the cabin roof. And if we had been black before, it was nothing to what we soon became. The greasy, fluffy muck descended upon our heads, which, lacking sou'westers, we could not properly protect.

The "Dundases" came and looked at us, and their Number One came aboard and kindly offered to help, but we reckoned this was our own particular load of grief and that they ought to keep out of it until we had got a little further.

For nine days we worked on the ship. Supper was made late, for we could work on the cabin by lamplight, and while we worked we were filthy, so that it was no use stopping until we were prepared to finish for the day and begin the long process of cleaning up. This we did not do until we were too tired to go on any longer. At any moment a fresh cargo might arrive, or a visiting authority take a notion to come and look at us. Naval Control, Scrabster, must know what had happened, and would, we hoped, soft-pedal their answers to any enquiry from Thurso; but there was always the chance of a stranger who knew not Joseph. So we got on with it. When we had cleaned off all the muck, the First Officer of the *Dundas* remade the partition and bookcase for us.

By the time the new paint had been put on, the *Dundas* had finished loading and was ready to sail. We went aboard her in the evening to thank them all for what they had done.

The Skipper did not drink, and did not say much. He was a small man, with a worn face that looked gravely past our careless youth to the thing that might have happened, and anxiously from this war and his long service at sea towards his retirement with his family at Brixham. The war had come before he could build his house.

"But I've bought me land," he affirmed, as though that were a fact which no disaster could shake. And from time to time he would repeat, in a low tone of finality, "I've bought me land!"

10

SPRING RUNS

"Billow and breeze
Mountains and seas
Islands of rain and sun!"
—*Sing me a song...*

BETWEEN THE 26th February and the 22nd April we did seven runs.

Not much, perhaps, for nearly two months, but the limiting factors were numerous and, literally, vital. Dr Worth, who had sized up the situation after two or three passages, had prescribed "favourable conditions and proper management", and most of our waking time was spent in trying to find out whether the conditions could, by any stretch of the imagination, be described as favourable, and to see that the management was proper. Concentration upon these matters was so continuous and intense (in view of the penalties involved) that we soon worked without any conscious calculation whatever; and gradually we realised that in such conditions there grows an awareness that has nothing to do with the ordinary senses.

We found that, barring accidents, the average of one return trip every ten days could be maintained. I do not know how long we could have gone on with it. A fifteen-ton boat is rather large for two people to handle in any sort of crisis; and we did not make things any easier for ourselves by doing our own loading and unloading.

Yet those two months of the early spring of 1940 were, I believe, the best we ever spent. There were practically none of the dreary complications which follow an organisation of any size. There were simply two people running one small boat with single, definite cargoes, at more or less regular intervals. Our problems were all either natural or mechanical: of time, weather, and tide, of sails and engine, of food and sleep. And all round was a glory of sea and cliff and sky, with their everlasting wonder of change and detail.

Our work began to settle down, as we had always hoped it would, and to pay dividends. But there was never any question of monotony!

25th February. A further load of gelignite arrived at Thurso while we were obliterating the traces of the fire. Also a cheerful and kindly letter from Cooke, and one not so cheerful from Harrison, forwarding one to them from Hutchinson, which seems to show that our standing as carriers is still shaky. The Lyness people want supplies of gasless delay-action detonators (whatever those may be), which Cooke's are not making at present but can make if required. I am to see Hutchinson in a day or two, when he visits Lyness. I shall imply that anything he cares to ask shall be provided, on condition that we carry it!

We took the gelignite across today. There was a westerly swell which was unpleasant for an hour or so off Dunnet, but the tide was with it and drew its teeth.

After unloading we were told by Jervis that the contract was again short of detonators and that he had wired for three more cases to be sent from Invergordon. Did we think we could fetch them speedily? We said we would try.

2nd March. Fortunately the weather has held. We got back to Scrabster on the 27th, loaded the detonators the same night, and crossed with them on the 28th.

Off-loaded yesterday. This seems to have cheered Jervis up considerably. Back to Scrabster today in lovely calm weather. Margaret knitting a red jersey against time all the way back, since we are bidden to Thurso Castle tonight and are short of garments. Engine leaking at cooling-water joints.

At tea tonight with the Sinclairs, Norton asked us in

public how much we were getting paid for carting the explosives. When I told him, he remarked "You must be making a lot of money!"

All the way home, Margaret and I were thinking of the things we might have said in answer to that one. Our total receipts to date were £183, of which £90 went to pay debts incurred on the journey north, and £20 was chargeable solely to ship's expenses, such as petrol, dues, ship's gear, and so on, during the two months we had been based at Scrabster. The balance of £73 would not have paid us each, weekly, since we started this show, the wages of a deckhand in a drifter.

The risks we were taking were physically considerable and financially appalling, and we were living in what most people would have described as gross discomfort. After another year of it, we came to envy keenly the drifter crews the warmth and power of their boats, their regular pay, and their exemption from financial worries. "Danger" money, "hard-lying" money, and "overtime" were luxuries that the Union of Merchant Adventurers unfortunately could not press for.

14th March. To Lyness with more detonators, chocked off thoroughly, if incongruously, by twenty bags of potatoes. Spring tides. We were one hour and thirty-five minutes between Holburn Head and Cantick Light, which is eighteen miles in a straight line. The average speed was nearly twelve knots over the ground. It was a glorious, roaring run, that provoked much song and mirth and high spirits.

Being in before lunch, we off-loaded this afternoon. But the days are still too short to think of a return journey before dark. Besides, the westerly wind that bowled us here so merrily will create a very different state of affairs on the ebb tide. The Merry Men will be dancing tonight.

15th March. Last night Margaret dreamt of lice—a hereditary phenomenon in her family, which portends disaster. We both woke to a feeling of unease, which grew, without any ascertainable reason, throughout the day.

Just at dusk, when we were thinking hopefully about supper and Margaret had set a Primus going, something seemed to hit the ship like a blow from a very large hammer. No doubt there was a noise, but the shock was a concussion rather than a noise. It was so severe that the thought flashed across my mind that we had done it at last—blown up our cargo and probably half Lyness as well—until I remembered that we had unloaded yesterday.

When we had established that the ship was still afloat, apparently unharmed, we tumbled out into the cockpit.

Everything outside seemed perfectly normal. The *Greenwich*, the big storeship moored close by, lay quiet and unmoved. The wind had died away, and nothing disturbed the serenity of the evening except a faint murmur of aircraft engines. We saw presently a twin-engined bomber moving slowly overhead into the velvet glow which still lingered in the west.

Then, suddenly, streams of tracers filled the sky from a score of points on the surrounding islands. The beams of searchlights sprang out and switched to and fro across the dark. More noise of engines rose with the crack of gunfire. Something spun close over us that sounded like a cat whose tail had been trodden on.

I called to Margaret to go below and lie on one of the bunks, until we knew what all this was about. Our planks would not be much use against a stray bullet, but the bunks, being below the waterline, might give a better chance. We were still not at all clear what was happening. We had never been in an air raid, and were under the impression that they always began with the warning siren, with whose infernal wail we were familiar enough. But there had been no warning, and we had a lingering idea that this sudden Brock's benefit was no more than a practice.

The racket nearby soon subsided. Far away over Flotta, an aircraft, tiny and white as a toy, slid down the beam of a searchlight until it met the outline of the hill, where its disappearance was succeeded by a dull glow.

We fed, and speculated, and went to bed. Next morning, I heard at the Drifter Office that the cruiser *Norfolk* had been hit in the fo'c'sle and fourteen men killed. The bump that we had felt was from a bomb that had fallen between us and the *Greenwich*. We told each other that it must have been aimed at us, with the obvious intention of setting off our load and destroying Lyness—an idea which we found disturbing, but satisfactory!

16th–20th March. Wind! Good Lord, I have never seen such wind. I did not think it possible that mental balance could be so assailed by a mere movement of air. It came, under a grey, hard sky, from the south-east, and grew through thirty-six hours to a screaming fury of pressure.

We were first roused to action in the early hours of the morning by the sickening shock of the *Mermaid* snubbing on her anchor-chain against the big can buoy of the mooring. We had paid out ten fathoms of it—as much scope as we dared give her in that small space—but she was pulling it straight on the tops of considerable waves which were piling up over the two-mile drift from Flotta. We had to double it—an operation which put us to the limits of our strength for about four hours.

There was no possibility of pulling her or driving her up to the buoy. We had to use the dinghy—hauled, hand over hand, along the chain—to pass, first of all, a doubled four-inch grass rope and a doubled hemp warp of the same size to the ring of the buoy. These held the ship—still snubbing hideously, but with a less unyielding thump— whilst the end of the chain was brought back.

By that time, the wind, unbelievably, had increased, and the *Mermaid* had begun to snub again, pulling the doubled sixty-foot lengths of her half-inch cable into straight lines as the seas and the wind pressure on her tall mast hove her back bodily from the buoy.

In the beginnings of the dawn we loaded our two lorry tyres into the dinghy, hauled the dinghy out once more along the chain, and lashed the tyres in the bight of it, using three-quarters of our effort to prevent the dinghy capsizing or being pinned under the chain.

The tyres did the trick. Their combined weight was a hundred and sixty pounds, and, half-submerged, they held another forty or fifty pounds of water, making a soggy buffer that the ship could not lift. Yet all the time the wind was increasing—far beyond anything we had known or imagined.

The first and worst stage of the storm reached its peak that afternoon. We were shuffled out of sleep at about three o'clock by the maniac din outside and by the violent pitching of the ship.

It was as well we had made an adequate job of the mooring in good time, because we could have done very little about it now. The scene that met us as we poked our heads through the door of the cockpit was like something from another planet. The atmosphere above Ore Bay was filled to an unknown height with a disintegrated mass of water, which was driving in sheets and vortices towards the head of the bay. The shore there, although only a quarter of a mile away, was invisible. The *Greenwich*, about a cable distant, showed only as a dim shape through the smother. Large, white-crested seas, raised in only two miles of drift, raved past, their smoking tops level with the deck. A diving-boat, about fifty feet long, moored immediately astern of us, was showing half its bottom as it reared over the seas.

Our tyres seemed to be doing their job. They would lift as each wave swept under the *Mermaid*, until the double bight of the chain, wrapped inboard round mast and winch, was nearly straight, but always their weight kept a slight sag in it and prevented that final snub, which, before we put them there, had threatened to snap the chain or drag the winch-bolts out of the deck.

In the marvellous, though uneasy, patch of calm that was the cabin, we sat or lay for hours, fretted by anxiety, unable to eat or sleep, or concentrate on anything but the appalling pressures outside.

During the war we had only occasional reports of the figures of wind speed in Orkney. On one occasion an anemometer at Lyness went off the scale at 110 m.p.h. and broke. Since the war a speed of 130 m.p.h. has been recorded. I am sure that more than once at Lyness we rode out gales of upwards of 90 m.p.h. By all appearances, this may have been one of them.

On the third day it subsided gradually, before blowing up again from the west.

At last, on the 20th, we got away. Lacking any agent at Scrabster we could never tell whether a fresh cargo had arrived in our absence, and a prolonged delay always put us in a fret to get back and find out.

Coming back, we were thrown about a good deal in the middle of the Firth by the tail of the Men of Mey race, which had not quite subsided. A big destroyer passed eastwards at speed—a stately and stirring sight, though it was two or three miles away. Half an hour later, we sighted breaking water stretching across our bows in a single steep-sided wall, that looked about eight feet high. It did not move; and not until the *Mermaid* had taken it with a heart-shaking heave and crash, and we found nothing but quiet water beyond, did we realise that it was the destroyer's bow wave, that had been lying up against the tide and breaking steadily, all that time.

Before we got in, it had already started to pipe up again from the east. In a bitter, sleet-laden wind, we sailed the ship into her berth, glad, as always, to get home. An engineer from a small tug that was lying weather-bound on the south wall came aboard us, and, seeing us both wet after the passage, tore off his duffel coat and insisted on Margaret's accepting it. A nice gesture, and the only literal example I have seen of "giving the coat off his back!"

21st March. It was as well we got back as soon as possible. There was a cargo in the station, and a message from

Norton to say that it must be removed at once. Owing to
the recent air activity he wanted it out of there. We telephoned to our friend Andrew Swanson, the lorry owner,
and his drivers brought it down and helped to stack it on
the quay beside *Mermaid*'s berth.

There were some kind enquiries about the raid. We
resisted the temptation to spin a good yarn, remembering
in time that raids were yet another threat to the confidence
of the public in the presence of several tons of explosive.

The east wind having failed to develop seriously in the
face of a rising glass, we loaded the cargo and got away at
three-forty-five, as early as the tide allowed. Switha seven
p.m. Moorings seven-forty-five. A black, cold evening, with
rain, and the glass turning downwards again.

25th March. This day was a Friday and we made an
Error of Judgment, but were lucky enough to get away
with it. After holding us at Lyness the past three days with
strong winds, the weather has turned fine again—as fine as
it can only be in this place of furies. The luxury of warm
sunshine must have led us astray—that, and the fact that
the return tide did not begin until the afternoon.

The news that the Switha Gate was temporarily closed
for repair did not disturb me unduly, for we were up to
time on our shipments; but when the duty officer suggested
we go out by the Hoxa Gate instead, the usual urge to
return while the weather was fine came uppermost in my
mind, and I said we would.

It took me until I had got back to the ship to realise that
I had made a very silly decision. The Hoxa boom was away
on the other side of Flotta, in the south of the main part of
the Flow. To go that way would add five miles to the journey. We might just scrape home before the flood tide began,
but if anything happened to hold us up we should be out
for the night; and the weather could never be trusted in
these parts at this time of the year for as long as eighteen
hours.

The afternoon tallied so perfectly with our idea of

Paradise that these mundane considerations failed to weigh
with us as they should. We pushed off, and swam clamorously through floors of blazing mother-of-pearl, round
strange island corners into seas unknown to us.

The Hoxa boom seemed an infernally long way away.
It came into sight as a black line shimmering in a luminous
blank between the upturned ends of islands. For a long
time this line was broken only by the twin blobs of the two
boomships. At length, other blobs appeared along it, which
were the buoys. Urgently we approached the gap, expecting to see, as at Switha, the intervening buoys begin to
draw together away from the starboard ship.

Instead, a voice blaring through a loud hailer told us
to heave to. Considerably put about, I drove the wedge
behind the clutch lever and ground the propeller into
reverse. Then, leaving Margaret to keep the machine tick-
ing over, I went on deck, out of range of its interruptive
noises, and parleyed with the captain of the boomship.

Whether he had received a signal from A.C.O.S. to open
for us I don't know. He kept us waiting for over twenty
minutes before the drum on his quarter started turning
and grudgingly left us a few clear feet of water.

The time was now half-past four, and there were only
three hours of ebb left, and not a breath of wind to help
the engine.

Off Dunnet, in a dusk which would have been moth
haunted if it had been less keenly cold, the *Mermaid* gradu
ally drew to a stop. The engine ticked and pounded un
falteringly, all joints mercifully tight for once, and there
was a steady break of water from the bows which sent a
long barb of ripples away on either hand until they were
lost in shell-like gloom. But the whole darkening opalescen
sheet of water was moving inexorably and with increasing
speed in the wrong direction.

We were wondering when we should turn round, and
just which exiguous shelter we should try to lie in for the

night, when we became an object of interest to a patrol trawler.

It was one of the big Cape-class trawlers, a beautiful, powerful ship, with a cruiser stern and flaring bows like a destroyer's.

I daresay her captain took in the situation at once. But he was a tactful man. For at least a quarter of an hour we discussed the weather, the war, the price of petrol, sailing, and the sea-going qualities of the *Cape Portland*.

At last he suggested that it was a damned cold night and that if we would like to get to bed he could offer us a pluck into Thurso Bay, out of the tide. We passed the end of our warp—with what secret relief I need not describe—and he began to tow us at half speed: about nine knots.

The *Mermaid* sat on her tail, and the water rose to her rail and roared glassily asunder, as though it were the parting of the Red Sea.

Very gradually the outline of Dunnet changed direction and began to go backwards instead of forward.

The lighthouse had been abreast of us when the *Cape Portland* took us in tow, and the time was then eight p.m. We had some idea of what the tide had been when, at ten-thirty, she dropped our line a cable or two from Scrabster harbour, and we crept in, thankful, and cramped with cold. For the distance from Dunnet Light to Scrabster pier-heads is just six miles!

31st March. Four tons brought over yesterday. Whilst unloading this morning, the yellow raid warning went off, followed shortly by the red. Half the load was on the jetty, the other half still on board.

The rule was, that when a warning was sounded, all craft at the jetty cast off and stood away until the All Clear. This morning, everyone in our neighbourhood obeyed this order with unusual alacrity. We began casting off, too; but as we were about to leave, an officer came flying down from the Drifter Office and shouted to us to hold on.

Following hard on his heels came another officer, who told us to go away at once, as far as possible.

Apparently A.C.O.S. could not make up its mind whether to keep the two halves of our cargo together and chance one large bang, or to separate them and chance two lesser bangs.

In the ensuing flap, Margaret, who was alternately fastening and throwing off warps, got left waist-deep on the steps of the jetty, whilst I described small circles in the offing, unable, owing to the wind and the noise of the engine (which I could not leave) to make out exactly what was required of me. Just then the guns on Flotta opened up, and Captain Jermayne himself appeared on the jetty and waved to me to come back. No aircraft were seen over Lyness, and presently the All Clear went and we finished our job.

That morning, however, one thing seemed to lead to another. By the time we had finished, it was blowing quite hard from the west—hard enough, in fact, to make it impossible for our engine, which was not having one of its good days, to push the Mermaid bows first up to the buoy. There was so much windage on the mast that the head kept falling off before Margaret could pass the line. I could not help her, being unable to leave tiller and engine. After several attempts, she was dragged off the bows, clinging to the boathook, with which she had got hold of the buoy ring, but could not hold the ship.

She claimed ever afterwards that my only reaction to seeing her come floating aft was to ask her in no sympathetic tone of voice what she was doing there! She was on board again in very quick time. We then made a stern first approach up wind, which worked better.

Our proud boast that we were in sail in this war was proved hollow at the root by the necessities of time and economics. The engine—we had to admit—was the centre piece of our job. It always went, given sufficient nursing. We could have done better, perhaps, with a better engine

...ut we could not have done at all, without an engine of
...me kind. We should never have been allowed to kedge
...he *Mermaid* out of her berth whilst an admiral, in a
...innacle capable of thirty knots, waited in the offing!

At such times, when I had got the thing started and my-
...lf into my customary jack-in-the-box ballet between
...hrottle, gear lever, and tiller, the stately farewell measure
...f Sir Walter Raleigh seemed to parody itself through the
...proar in an infernal jig:

> "Even such is Time, that takes in trust
> Our youth, our joys, our all we have
> And pays us but with oil and rust . . . !"

April 1st–5th. Two raids and three gales, in five days.

The raids were confined to the main part of the Flow
...nd did not come our way. The battle-wagons have come
...n from the western sea-lochs, and the Luftwaffe seems to
...now all about it. Rumour has it that a gentleman has
...een apprehended ashore after sending a telegram through
...he Fleet Mail Office giving details of all the big ships in
...he Flow. It seems quite possible. We were rather discon-
...rted ourselves at about this time to find that a parcel of
...roceries which Margaret had bought at the N.A.A.F.I.
...ore at Lyness was wrapped in a chart of the Flow giving
...he positions of the Fleet moorings—whether out of date
...r not we did not know.

Security is really a frame of mind, and the frame of mind
...f nearly everybody is still too much in the picnic stage.

The gales raged according to pattern. A raid warning
...ent off in the middle of one of them, and the barrage bal-
...ons were sent up. The one nearest us was struck by light-
...ing and subsided, porpoising madly, in a plume of flame.
...nother dragged its attendant winch-lorry into the sea.

18th April. Another four tons of "jam". Greatly daring,
...e have hired a loader to help us shift these interminable
...xes from the quay to the *Mermaid*'s cabin. He is only
...rt-witted. I showed him how to put two boxes into the

rope sling, being particularly careful to keep the hook over the flat of a box, so that the sling would grip at the edges. Not a dozen hoists had come aboard when he forgot about this and let the hook slip to the edge.

The two boxes were off the ground and swinging inboard when I saw them up-end abruptly in the sling. Before I could do any more about it, they fell out, and dropped six feet on to the *Mermaid*'s side deck, upon which they burst with a sodden crunch.

Acquaintances in and about Scrabster who knew our business were often assuring us heartily that you could throw gelignite about as though it were jam, without any fear of its exploding. After looking cautiously about to make sure that none of these characters had witnessed the performance, I began to think they might be right. At least sometimes right. Demonstrably, either it did, or it didn't.

22nd April. Whilst ferrying this day a total of ninety-six thousand detonators (what on earth is Jervis going to do with that lot!) in eight cases, we were stopped in the Firth by a destroyer, who sent away a boarding party fully armed, in a cutter, to see what we were up to. She also trained a gun on us.

We had just finished lunch; and, what with backing and filling in none too good a humour in obedience to the destroyer's signals, we had forgotten to clear up. The boat came smartly alongside, the crew eyeing Margaret with commendable restraint. Her sub-lieutenant climbed into our cockpit, slightly flushed, and I showed him our papers.

He could hardly believe it. I followed him down into the cabin and we both stopped aghast before a sordid little of dirty plates, a bottle of limejuice, a loaf of bread, and a half-empty pot of jam, dotted amongst the clamps a sombre bank of Messrs Nobel's red-painted stout detonator cases. He said hastily "That's all right. Hold on will you, till I report," and went rapidly away.

In a mixture of mirth and confusion we watched the cutter hoisted on board, the sub. hasten to the bridge, a a movement of heads and binoculars. The gun turned fore-and-aft. "Carry on!" came a voice over the loud hailer. "Sorry to have delayed you! Good luck!"

It is said that if your work takes you daily up and down the Haymarket you will sooner or later meet everyone you ever knew. Scapa Flow in the war was rather like that.

At Scrabster, one old friend had already breakfasted with us by the light of *Mermaid*'s cabin lamp before crossing by the *St Ninian* to Lyness to pilot the minelayers laying the Iceland barrage.

In April, the destroyer *Griffin* came in from Norway for forty-eight hours to blow down her boilers, and we found that between us we knew no fewer than seven of those aboard. After we had spent a memorable evening with them, John Randall, the ship's doctor, obtained twenty-four hours' leave and sailed back with us.

John and I used to crew together in ocean races before the war in a boat called *Phryna*, named after an Athenian lady of no great virtue. Her rival was the R.A. Yacht Club boat *Rose*, an old gaff cutter, sailed very hard by a crew of Gunners, of which Bill Tarrant was usually a member. As we reached Scrabster, there ran in my head the disreputable chorus with which *Phryna*'s crew used to greet *Rose*'s entry into harbour:

> "Poor old *Rose*, she ain't what she used to be,
>   Ain't what she used to be,
>   AIN'T what she used to be!
> Poor old *Rose*, she ain't what she used to be
>   Long, long years ago!"

As we disembarked, John said:

"Now, Tony, where did you say Bill's to be found?"

"Here, in the transit shed. That door, where the sentry is."

"Sentry," said John, "I want you to take this message in to Captain Tarrant. Don't tell him I'm here. Just say this —that there's a woman outside with a baby in her arms, who wishes to speak to him!"

John looked at me without expression. A Faeroe gansey was stretched tightly round his large chest. A pair of my fearnoughts ended just below his knees, and a hiatus of bare leg showed above a pair of my rubber boots, which had suffered in the fire and had been cut down until they were not much more than goloshes. A red spade beard completed the effect.

Bill appeared in the doorway, saw John, and then had to stand and listen while John did his little act: "You would 'ave your will o' me!" and "Look what you brought me to!" (displaying the goloshes!)—while the sentry went purple in the face.

There was a party that night. Moignard, the lieutenant-commander in charge at Scrabster, joined us and drove us in to Thurso. John had to come as he was, since his uniform had been wrecked and his new one was not ready. The ladies of the hotel raised a collection for him, thinking that he was a Norwegian refugee. He must have confirmed this impression in their minds by charming his way to the kitchen, after a five-course dinner, and cooking himself a large plate of scrambled eggs.

I shall never forget the warmth and comradeship of that evening—the sheer delight of being with old friends with whom one has shared—and is sharing—an adventure. Food and wine made their bow, no doubt, but could not obtrude upon the hour.

And afterwards, what harbour was it, what mast, shining in the night, that witnessed our return? And what moonlit quay, watched by a silent sentry, could this be, that so gave back the echo of a remembered song? A song I had heard sung along the quays of what I could hardly believe was already another world:

> "My name is *Phryna*!
> Her name is *Rose*!
> We are two ladies—
> I don't suppose!"

11

TRIAL TRIP

"Grans estoit et mervellex et lais et hidex."
"Tall was he and great of growth, laidly
and marvellous to look upon."
Aucassin and Nicolette (Andrew Lang's translation)

THE PRESIDENT took the half-pint gin bottle that
Jock McKeown passed to him, knocked the neck off
against the *Briarbank*'s bulwark, poured the contents
down his throat, and pitched the bottle into the harbour.

The audience on the quay watched this performance
with admiration. Except for McCallum, Agent for Burns
Chalmers, one of the big Orkney contractors, who wore a
camel-hair coat and tweed cap, we were all in shirt sleeves.
There were Swanson's two lorry drivers, Edward and Willy
Beg, and Jock McKeown, fish and coal handler and owner
of another lorry which had been pressed into service by
McCallum to help load his cargo into our new ship. And
there was John Carr, an Ulsterman, our new partner from
the south, who wore a Jaeger hat tilted slightly to the back
of his head, its brim turned down over his round face,
making a little shadow from which his blue eyes looked
humorously at the world.

We had set up for shipowners.

Two people in *Mermaid* were not enough. Any accident
—even a bad cold—might mean a delayed cargo. At the
same time, *Mermaid* by herself could not earn enough
money to support more than two people.

But general cargo was piling up. Enemy bombers were
now so busy in the North Sea, and losses there were mounting to such an extent, that there were urgent enquiries for

shipment from Scrabster of anything that could be handled
by the Thurso–Inverness railway.

Being bound by our contract with Harrison, of which
nobody, official or private, showed the smallest signs of
wishing to relieve us, it seemed that we could not pack up.
Nor did we want to. We would have tried, on the strength
of what we had done so far, to get back into the Services,
if we could have stayed at sea. But we felt pretty certain
that, at that stage, women and cripples would still be
considered unfit to handle boats.

The only alternative was to expand, and incur all the
consequences of a business—a bigger ship, more money, a
partner. It was stupid, of course. Yet it seemed the obvious
thing to do. It seemed a logical and useful extension of
what we were doing already; and I thought then, being as
ignorant of shipping economics as I was of bureaucracy,
that, financially, if we did not stand to get rich, we could
hardly lose. The thought of being branded as profiteers
did not enter our heads. Whether, if it had, it would have
made any difference, I cannot honestly say; we had not got
used, at that time, to being hit harder by our friends than
by the sea or the enemy. I hope we should have said: "To
hell with it! Let us get on with the job!" We were utterly
absorbed in what we were doing, and the work was at that
time made vastly easier by our being still innocent enough
to believe that it might be considered worth while.

With John's consent I had already bought a Fifie called
Harvester, lying at St Monance on the Firth of Forth, and
was wondering how long it would take to convert her for
cargo, when I heard of this *Briarbank*, a sixty-ton Belgian
steel trawler, for sale in Wick. She was a hideous-looking
craft, with a dented stern and a huge semi-diesel engine.
But she was near at hand, and she had been converted for
cargo by a Lancashire scrap merchant, who had been running scrap in her to Aberdeen from wrecks in Orkney and
return cargoes of coal from Kirkwall. So we bought her, too.

All this, so far as my share was concerned, on borrowed

money! My passion for boats was somewhat cooled by the size of the outlay. I felt rather like the aqua-lung diver who goes beyond the safety depth and becomes afflicted with "ivresse des profondeurs", a condition described by Captain Cousteau as "a gaseous attack upon the nervous system".

Since eight o'clock on this perfect spring morning, we had been loading sleepers and pipes as fast as three lorries could bring them from Thurso. Jim Barnwell, *Briarbank*'s former owner, had lent us the crew for this first trip. Kenneth Edmondson, the engineer, and Jockie, the boy, had gone up to Mother Mackay's for their mid-morning pint, and the skipper, George McKay—"the President", as John had christened him—sat alone in the sunshine on a pile of hatchboards beside *Briarbank*'s open hatch, sweating profusely, in a state of sombre content.

Jock McKeown looked down at him, took a pull from a quart bottle of old-and-mild, and said benignly:

"Tea's a recht drink for a man to work on!"

"Naebody kens that better than yoursel'," rumbled the President, drawing a massive flipper across his moustache.

"Man," began Jock again, in tentative indignation, "ye ken it's forty year since I first clapped een on ye, and syne I've never touched a drop. Ye're an awfu' example."

"'At man," he went on, turning his fiery face to us in an audible aside, "'at man was once the richest man i' Wick!"

The President looked up at him without expression. "Ye may say so, ye b——, wha ha' spent yer days i' pubs on gold ye ha' robbit fra poor fishermaan!"

The conversation was continued with perfect good humour and understanding until Kenneth and "Chokie" returned, rather hurriedly, and we resumed loading.

Kenneth had used the winch for the sleepers, but the pipes, if handled in bundles, showed an uncomfortable tendency to slide, so we had been loading them singly with a hand purchase and rope strop.

The President was formed by nature for this particular job. He could grasp the fall of the purchase, take up the slack, and then make the motion of sitting down. He must have weighed twenty stone, and no load could resist the counterpoise of that enormous bottom. The eighteen-foot pipes leapt from the lorries. It was all the guymen could do to keep them in charge. When Kenneth, lean and keen as the blade of a knife, swung from quay to ship by the rigging, Jock McKeown was heard to remark "Weel, ye couldna do that, Geordie!"

"Na," admitted the President, complacently. "Ma strength's in ma arse, no in ma arrms!"

By four o'clock, the forehold was full. The hatchboards were put on, and the side decks filled to the top of the bulwarks with the rest of the pipes.

Then a thirty-hundredweight tractor appeared. Kenneth started his winch, rigged a double wire purchase and a spider's web of slings, and with the ship listing ten degrees plucked the tractor off the deck of the lorry. With four hands on one guy and the President on the other, the load was inched over the forehatch. Kenneth grimly braked it down in a series of jerks, which caused it to jump like a yo-yo, shook me to my soul, and evoked even from the President a mild grunt of warning. To Kenneth all things seemed possible.

We were not done yet. There were still three hundred camp beds to take aboard, besides a five-ton load of gelignite. These we loaded into the afterhold till past ten o'clock.

At last the drivers swapped a final jest and said goodnight, and we watched them take their lorries up the long slant towards Thurso, and bed. Quiet descended upon the little harbour. It was still broad daylight—the wonderful quiet gloaming of the northern summer.

We were sticky and exhausted, and had acquired a special grime that the *Mermaid* did not produce—even from her engine. It came from the coal dust, from which no square inch of *Briarbank* was free.

We felt a certain ragged sense of achievement, but the day's work had been brutish and long-drawn. It left me with a profound respect for Kenneth's cynical mastery of the crude and the monstrous, and—for I was very tired—a dull misgiving that, without him, we had bitten off more than we could chew. We turned gratefully along the quay in the still afterglow towards the *Mermaid*. Never, than as she lay there so quietly in the silken shadow of the wall, did she seem more like home!

Next day, the 8th May, the sun rose upon as perfect a morning as the last had been. It was the beginning of a spell of weather that was to last, in the north, unbroken until the end of June: "Dunkirk weather"—a time, for England, of salvation snatched from disaster by a miracle, the time that saw Germany on the move against us, and the nation compelled at last to give Mr Churchill the chance of doing something about it.

Since, after this trip, we should be trying to run the ship ourselves, John and I took the chance of trying to learn something about the engines. We forsook the sunshine, to spend long spells in the thunderous cavern of the engine-room, moving cautiously in Kenneth's wake over the oily footplates between the fuel tanks and the great shaking cylinders, while he displayed the monster and its accessories and explained how simple it was.

"She's *got* to go!" he reiterated. In starting the machine, you opened the compression cocks, pulled the flywheel over to the starting position, primed the cylinders, lit the blow-lamps. When a curl of blue smoke appeared from the compression cocks, you closed them, turned off the lamps, opened the air starting-valve with a quick turn of the wrist —and off she went. It was as easy as that.

There were, however, little humours in the machine which were worth attending to. As he pointed them out, with a kind of cynical terseness, it appeared to us that it

was only too easy to do one's self or the ship serious injury
by quite small oversights. For instance, the crowbar used
for pulling the flywheel over to the starting position could,
by premature ignition, be sent through the side of the ship
or the operator's head. And it was quite possible, by for-
getting to open the oil drain-cocks in the sump, to cause
the engines to race uncontrollably—a prospect I found
difficult to contemplate, seeing that the flywheel weighed
four tons!

Casually, under persistent interrogation, Kenneth came
to another little matter whose implications, when at length
we grasped them, struck us as simply appalling.

In order to explain why, I am afraid it is necessary to
be a little technical.

The engine was a two-stroke semi-diesel machine with
two cylinders, firing by compression. We had learnt by this
time that it was started by compressed air. The air was
stored in two large steel tanks or bottles, fixed to the forward bulkhead. From these a pipe led to a stop-valve on the
after (No. 2) cylinder. The stop-valve was opened and shut
by a short hand lever, rather like the handle of the door
of a car. Upon the manner in which you opened and shut
this valve your very life might depend.

Opening the valve admitted air from the bottles at high
pressure into No. 2 cylinder. This punched No. 2 piston
downwards. The idea was that No. 1 piston then came up
with sufficient impetus to carry it over the top of its stroke
and fire No. 1 cylinder. Whereupon it, in its turn, forced
No. 2 piston up and over and caused No. 2 cylinder to fire;
and off they both went.

This happy outcome depended entirely upon the length
of time the air-starting valve was held open by the operator.

If he shut it too soon, not enough air would go in to
punch No. 2 piston down to the bottom and No. 1 piston
over the top. No 1 cylinder might then not fire at all. Or,
it might backfire and the engine would then start turning
comfortably but uselessly in the wrong direction.

The disaster was to hold the valve open too long. The piston would then go down and uncover the exhaust port before the valve was closed. Result: the contents of the bottles would then rush through the cylinder and away through the exhaust.

Now, the reason why this was so extremely serious was that the bottles themselves could only be charged *whilst the engine was running*. They were charged by back-pressure from No. 2 cylinder. *There was no auxiliary compressor*. And the bottles, fully charged, contained air only for three starts. Miss it three times, or miss it, badly, once, and the *Briarbank* became, in the words of Kipling's McAndrew, "a log upon the sea"!

In the sunlit wheelhouse, the President gripped the spokes of the wheel and hearkened to the thump of the engine with morose contempt. To him it was nothing but a noise, which, in some manner, made the ship go. So long as it remained constant, he ignored it. If it altered, or if the large clutch lever beside the wheel required to be moved, as, of course, it did on entering or leaving harbour, he betrayed signs of alarm and bellowed hoarsely for Kenneth.

The compass, slung in the roof above his head, concerned him as little as the engine. He was steering now by keeping his eye generally upon the place he wanted to go to. As we drew nearer to the South Walls of Hoy, it became clear that this target was Cantick Sound. I murmured to him what I felt sure he knew already: that Cantick was mined. But the amateur was disregarded, and it took all the persuasion of Kenneth, barking into his ear in a kind of Doric shorthand, to convince him that it really was necessary to leave Cantick alone and continue past the point of Switha. From this time on, the Presidential indignation began to mount.

At the examination vessel we were ordered through Hoxa. This meant an extra five miles round the back of

Flotta; and it was not until three o'clock that we reached
the wooden jetty at Lyness and pushed our way into a
crowded mass of drifters to discharge the gelignite. When
we had finished, drifters lay six deep outside us and a fresh
tier had formed astern.

The President, now quite congested, put the engine full
astern, grasped the wheel, and gazed ahead with a fixed
indomitable stare, while the water roared forward between
our imprisoned ship and her neighbours and Kenneth
grimly cast off every rope he could reach. Under these circumstances, something was bound to happen sooner or
later. Slowly, with many stops and bumps and unheeded
cries from the drifters, we ground our way backwards out
of the jam. I began to appreciate the advantages of an iron
vessel, and also to realise how the *Briarbank*'s stern had
acquired its peculiar shape.

The next move was to the stone quay to unload Burns
Chalmers's cargo. Here the congestion was even worse, and
here the traffic was of steel and much larger than we were,
so that Kenneth had to exercise a restraining influence
upon the skipper's single-mindedness. We spied our friend
the *St Angus*, a coaster chartered by Burns Chalmers, discharging huts, and tied up alongside her, while I went
ashore to find someone of Burns Chalmers's and ask for
a berth. Their foreman told us to wait until the *St Angus*
had finished and then to go inside her.

Through the zenith of the sweltering afternoon we
hovered about our ship, drinking tea, yarning sporadically
with the crew of the *St Angus*, and waiting for our deliverance. We could not rest, lest we should be forgotten, perhaps for days; and the business of keeping ourselves in the
foreground, and stating our case whenever there seemed
to be an opening, gave us no peace. Being paid for what
we did, not for the time that we spent in doing it, demur-
rage remained at our charge, not at the Government's. I
had not yet learned the comfortable way to arrange a war
contract.

Tom Ross, the *St Angus*'s skipper, was an Ulsterman from Portovogic, and he and John struck up a strong acquaintance. He expounded to John a long, ingenious argument: that the war had nothing to do with Hitler, but was due, in some way, to the machinations of the Pope.

At last, at about six o'clock, we were ordered round to the boom slip, inside the boom boats, and there, with long punctuations while the single lorry available disappeared with its loads, we discharged beds till midnight.

The piermaster then told us to shove off for the night. He was a retired lieutenant-commander, who had the reputation of cutting with an axe the warps of any ship which showed any reluctance to obey his orders. But it was late, and we were able to stall until he forgot us and disappeared.

At last the quay was deserted.

Covered with grime and sweat, and with feet so sore, it was a pain to move over the deckload of pipes, we descended into the empty afterhold, and there, treading delicately over a half-inch carpet of fine coal dust, we erected two of Burns Chalmers's camp beds, and sat on them carefully with our sailbags, whilst Margaret gallantly cooked something for us to eat.

We had had to bring, like tinkers, household gear sufficient for a week, and the labour of unpacking, passing, and placing this, whilst keeping it and ourselves clear of the coal dust, was ridiculous past belief. Gradually our somnambulist movements drew to the point where they could cease, and at last we were still, one in the wheelhouse and two amongst the coal dust beneath the grey square of the afterhatch, in which a group of stars seemed to look down at us in silent wonder.

During the next three days, we were chased from Lyness to Flotta, and back again to the *St Angus*, into which we at last discharged the dregs of our cargo. There were long delays, during which the President made noises like a volcano preparing to erupt, while Kenneth's face became

twisted into a strip of settled bitterness. After one long wait
and a last-minute cancellation of orders, the President
became so cross that without waiting for assistance he
started the ship full astern and bellowed for Kenneth to
deliver him. Only Chokie was happy. He was still at an
age when all roads seem to lead dead straight and slightly
downhill, and he passed his spare time whistling
dolorously, in perfect content.

Tom Ross gave us supper in the *St Angus* the night
before we left, and we heard the news that Belgium had
capitulated. We were all silent for a moment, unable to
grasp what this would mean, but stunned by what was
obviously a major and appalling disaster. And then John
smiled and said gently to Tom: "They'll be calling the
County Down Militia out next!"

Going back to Scrabster, we ran for the first time in ten
days beneath a grey sky and a cold wind.

The *Briarbank*'s owners took the wheel in turn. Kenneth brewed cups of tea at frequent intervals and passed
them round. The President kept below, and reappeared
only when he thought tea might be ready, most other
occasions being by now beneath his notice.

Soon after we had passed Dunnet and were bumping
through the incipient tide race, his walrus face and
Clemenceau moustaches appeared once more, framed in
the fo'c'sle hatch. He emerged slowly, moved aft past the
wheelhouse, and was seen to be relieving himself on deck
by the engine-room casing. My attention, drawn by John
to this proceeding, was diverted from steering the ship,
and as she sheered off course the top of a sea smacked over
the bulwark and caught the President fair and square.

I still have the bit of paper on which I wrote down the
President's address, when he left us at Scrabster at the end
of that week; and though I saw him once again before he
died with Barnwell on the rocks of South Ronaldshay, my

last memory of him is of his large form, dressed very neatly in a brown suit, and of his deep old face, beneath its cap, expressionless as ever, but somehow contented, as he waddled off along the quay.

Kenneth was to come to us again, and drive the *Briarbank* for many a month in his cynical, irresistible way.

Just now, at the end of our trial trip, the ship seemed cold and empty without them both.

12

DOG DAYS

"But oh, what a cruel thing is a farce to those engaged in it!"
Travels with a Donkey

EVEN AFTER the trial trip John and I were still under
the impression that we would have little difficulty in
running the *Briarbank* ourselves. She had had a crew
of three. We were a crew of three. I did not stop to realise
that if, say, the President and Kenneth had undertaken to
run the *Mermaid* in place of Margaret and myself, I should
have thought a long time before letting them try. A
thirteen-ton semi-diesel engine cannot be taken to pieces in
an afternoon. And without compressed air and plenty of
it there was no room for experiment.

We were in trouble even before we started. The air
pressure dropped while we lay in Scrabster, there being
what Kenneth had casually referred to as a "geeze" in some
joint or other; and after trying to top up from the
St Angus's bottles, via a diving hose which burst repeatedly,
we obtained only a half-hearted start. Half-hearted because,
in the middle of the Firth, we found the engine was running on only one cylinder.

It took us ten hours to reach Scapa. There, after discharging most of the cargo by hand, we lay for a week,
jammed amongst a mass of shipping, trying to borrow air,
and failing because of unsuitable hose and connections.
(Having been built in Belgium, the ship's connections
were all made with Continental threads and would not fit
British nuts and flanges.)

At last we were given a tow to Lyness, where, for want

of any other home, we made fast to Baldry's buoy. We had cargo for Barrow, the agent for James Fairbairn & Co., who was building a steel jetty at Lyness. Part of this we landed with the aid of Baldry's launch. A good deal of it had to remain on board. We apologised to Barrow as best we could, and, gathering up our household gear, crossed to Scrabster in the *St Ninian*.

At Scrabster the first discovery we made was that six boxes of gelignite had disappeared from the stack we had left on the quay. We were still using the *Mermaid* for explosives until we should feel a little happier about our ability to run the *Briarbank*, and had left this lot, covered with a tarpaulin well-roped round the middle, standing on the quay within ten yards of the sentry, to await our return.

There followed some of the worst hours I have ever spent. To mislay three hundred pounds of high explosive at such a place and time was rather more awful than to have mislaid the Crown Jewels. Yet it seemed utterly impossible that six boxes, each two feet long and weighing fifty pounds, could have been stolen within ten yards of an armed sentry, especially as the tarpaulin would have had to be removed and tied down again. And somehow I did not think they had been stolen. Everyone, from the sentries upwards, stalled at my questions with the maddening and rather obvious air of people who knew all about it but had been told to keep their mouths shut.

At last I was sent for by Norton, who solemnly announced that our six boxes had been buried by a party of sappers beneath the roadway on the bridge below Scrabster House, that invasion was expected at any moment, that I was to say nothing more about it, and that in future no more explosive was to be left on the quay.

"Dig a hole in the ground!" he suggested. "Or, what about that concrete building at Scrabster below the bridge?"

The building he referred to already contained the hydro-electric lighting plant for the village and the only approach to it was a goat track sloped at forty degrees. I had a fleeting vision of Mrs Mac's face when I should propose stacking four tons of gelignite along with our spare sails in the shed behind her house—literally the only place left in Scrabster for storing anything—and realised that there was nothing for it but to build a magazine.

It was through enquiries we made of Alec Sinclair, the assistant harbourmaster, for help in building our magazine, that his kinsman, James, presented himself to us one day at Scrabster. And so began an association, warm, amusing, and at times exasperating, which was to last for the next two years. James was wearing a new "Esso" boiler suit in butcher's blue-and-white stripes, and his big weather-beaten face lighted now and then with a quick little smile. With a further eye to the family main chance, he had brought with him his son, "Choorge". Most of that clan shared the disconcerting habit of lifting the corner of the upper lip when disagreeing at all in ordinary conversation—a habit we found invaluable when James came, later, to deal on our behalf with certain Water Transport officers from the St Magnus Hotel.

It was agreed that John should superintend the building of the magazine, while Margaret and I made a run in *Mermaid* with the gelignite.

"I'm sorry to leave you sweltering here ashore, John," I said. "This is going to be a holiday for us, after the *Briarbank*. But I think we had better take this lot before anyone else pinches some more of it. When we get back, and the magazine is done, we'll all go across in the Ninian and try to bring back that dreadful ship!"

"Give my regards to Barrow!"

"No fear! We're keeping clear of Barrow, until we can make *Briarbank*'s engine work!"

But when we came alongside at Lyness to discharge, we saw Barrow on the jetty. He watched the unloading in silence. Then he moved into the foreground, and became quietly interrogatory about his cargoes.

There were eight tons of pig iron and a ton and a half of paint for Fairbairn's still lying in *Briarbank*'s hold. Barrow hinted very nicely that we might discharge it now, using the *Mermaid* as a ferry.

We did not see how we could decently refuse!

Barrow sent a slow-spoken, broad-shouldered Lancashire-man named Tony off with us to help. Tony received his assignment in silence and with a reddening face.

We took the cover and boards off the afterhatch, rove a whip at the derrick, and started to sling seventy-pound drums of paint out of the hold and into *Mermaid*'s cockpit, whence they had to be handled into her cabin, being too wide to be lowered direct through the skylight. I see from our cargo book that there were forty-eight drums of paint, weighing 1 ton 11 hundredweights 2 quarters.

In the pitch and blaze of the afternoon we went back and started on the pig iron. Three hundred rusty pigs were slung out singly—for they weighed from thirty to sixty pounds apiece—and were stowed on *Mermaid*'s cabin floor, in the cockpit, and even on her side decks, until she wallowed under the load. By the time we had got them on to the jetty, it was nine o'clock.

We had had as much as we could stand. Since seven that morning, Margaret and I had ourselves handled, once, four tons of explosive, and with the help of one man had then handled twice—at least twice, since there was much fleet-ing and dragging in it—seven and a half tons of further cargo, the whole in average lifts of half a hundredweight. In the course of this, we had been on our feet practically continuously for fourteen hours. Barrow could now load the legs of his crane and get on with his jetty.

I felt heartily ashamed of myself for involving Margaret in such a performance. Fortunately we were fit enough to take no harm from it. We used to take rather a pride in the handling of our standard four-ton load. The appearance of *Mermaid* at the jetty was always the signal for a certain amount of haste, and we aimed at passing the last of our hundred and sixty fifty-pound boxes up through the sky-light and into the hands of Baldry's men within forty minutes of coming alongside. Jervis always had a team of six men ranged on the steps, with nothing to do but pass the boxes from one to another without moving their feet. Their ganger used to call a halt after the eightieth box, and we would feel impatient as we watched them getting their breath.

Barrow's pig iron introduced us to the depths. We finished that day in no buoyant spirit, but in an ache and stupor of body and a disgust of soul. Barrow very decently asked us up to his living quarters and gave us a bath and supper.

He exempted us next day from landing the remaining two tons. As things turned out, he never had need of it, and it lay for nine months in *Briarbank*'s hold, until she returned to Scrabster and it was lifted out on to the quay to make room for more urgent cargo.

The magazine was soon finished. We had chosen a spot on the lighthouse road, half way between the end of the village and the lighthouse, where it seemed a large explosion would do the least damage. John had tracked down and bought an old strong-room door from the manager of one of the Thurso banks. The hole in the braeside was lined with concrete and roofed with reinforced concrete and three feet of soil and turf. James finished off an excellent job by painting the door with a dull red-and-green camouflage and draping over it a piece of herring net stuck with sprigs of heather. From half a mile away the place was practically invisible.

When it was done, we turned our attention once more to the *Briarbank*.

The first necessity was to bring her back to Scrabster. Lying unmanned and unguarded at an inadequate mooring in Ore Bay, she would sooner or later be in trouble.

We packed up our pots and pans and bedding again, and crossed to Lyness in the *St Ninian*. There we found the

Cornucopia, a big seine-net boat fitted with a Bolinder 60-h.p. semi-diesel engine. Her skipper kindly agreed to come alongside in the evening and do what he could.

I must admit that by this time I was becoming morbid about these operations. I had a fixed determination to work on *Briarbank* if necessary till I dropped, but I felt that I wanted no witnesses to any further failures.

Of course, it only needs such a frame of mind in one of the actors of a piece to make comedy certain!

Nature had provided an evening of copper and gold, full of a hot, still glow, and gathered burning ripples slowly, from the smallest movement, into her infinity. She lapped even the battered form of the *Briarbank* in folds of light, glorified the mortals upon her deck, and received with entranced peace the indecent thudding of *Cornucopia*'s engine. I should have realised that one cannot charge air bottles, and get heated about it, in Arcadia!

The "Cornucopias" were in a happy frame of mind. Their mate was, curiously enough, an Italian, and he insisted upon our first going aboard and inspecting the ship. Presently Margaret informed me with shaking shoulders that, as the result of a delicate approach to John by the mate, she had been offered the freedom of *Cornucopia*'s lavatory. *Briarbank*'s deficiencies had immediately been noted by the Latin mind, which had reacted in its typical manner.

Soon afterwards, when our first hose blew out, the two youngest members of *Cornucopia*'s crew took it as a signal to ask me if they might borrow our dinghy to go fishing. I remembered, just in time, to tell them pleasantly that they could have it. They withdrew themselves from our ken. Vaguely, I was aware of shouts, as the Italian called them alongside, and then jovially soused a bucket of water at them before bidding them be off.

John was standing by in the engine room and I was patching the third burst in the pipe, when I heard Margaret say, appalled: "My God, here's Barrow!"

Tony's bunched shoulders, and the small, neat figure sitting upright and motionless in the stern of the dinghy, that grew upon us from the direction of the wooden pier, were unmistakable. There was no retreat. Margaret hissed in my ear: "Take no notice! Perhaps he won't come aboard."

But he came. And he brought his dog, Fiona, with him, and his deerstalker, and his shepherd's crook.

There was really no reason why he shouldn't have come: naturally, he wanted to see if the ship upon which he was relying for the transport of a good deal of his cargo could be made to go. But, besides feeling very guilty towards Barrow, we were in no humour just then to be asked, as we wiped the sweat out of our eyes, whether we were working hard. We must have been so obviously near our curse that he moved uncertainly away, poking at things with his stick, Fiona, highly nervous in such unfamiliar surroundings, cringing behind him.

Air was coming through at last. We leaned into the casing to confer with John, and learned that both bottles were up to 120, with everything holding, so far. On deck, the hose jumped apoplectically to the beat of *Cornucopia's* engine. Barrow and Fiona were regarding it—Barrow with doubt, Fiona with shivering apprehension. "A hundred and thirty-five!" called John.

It couldn't last. It was too old and too patched. I had felt all along that the ethos of the evening was not con-ducive to successful engineering operations.

The bang, when it came, was all that could have been desired. It was enormous, and final. For a second or two afterwards the air screamed out of a twelve-inch rent in the hose. The crew of *Cornucopia* cheered. Barrow dropped his stick. Fiona shot into the wheelhouse, found our bedding dumped there, and instantly performed upon it those rites by which little dogs invariably relieve themselves of an excess of nervous strain.

For the moment, there was nothing more that we could do.

I felt sick, and suddenly very weary, and when the "Cornucopias" asked us aboard for a drink I almost welcomed their kindness, though to my heated brain it seemed just another of that evening's conspiracies.

The skipper and the mate took us down into their snug cabin in the rounded stern. They gave us rum in mugs. Encouraged, no doubt, by Margaret's presence, our hosts were at the top of their form. The skipper produced a photograph of his twin daughters, which he passed round with pride. Then another photograph, showing a group of young women, one of whom, he explained, was his wife. He thrust the second photograph at Barrow, and, digging him jovially in the ribs, invited him in a hoarse whisper to see if he could "pick out the mother"!

Catching the eye of the *Cornucopia*'s saturnine engineer, who had witnessed this little act of the skipper's many times before, I left Barrow to his fate, and dived out to smoke a pipe in the engine room. As I went, I heard the skipper break into a roar of delighted laughter and saw him spill another three inches of rum into Barrow's mug.

Since the spy scare in Orkney during the winter, a curfew had been imposed. By eleven p.m. everyone was supposed to be indoors, except the military police. Offenders against this rule had been severely dealt with.

When at last we went on deck again, it was a quarter-to.

On *Briarbank*'s shoreward side there was no sign of Tony. For several minutes we sent roars, single and combined, across the hundred yards of shadow towards the wooden pier. Only the sentry, in time, answered, shouting back indignantly in the tone that is evoked by a late turn-out from a pub, that there was no one there, and that we had better pipe down and go to bed.

We thought of our own dinghy—and remembered that

it had been borrowed, years, as it seemed, before, by *Cornu-copia*'s two deckhands. A survey of the lake of waning light that was Ore Bay discovered a black blob afar off at the head of it in the shadow of the hills. How to make them hear? Desperately, we boarded again the silent *Cornu-copia*, from whose crew—all except the two wretched boys in our dinghy—the jollity of the evening was fast ebbing into sleep. After some minutes, the Italian came on deck, clad in his underpants, with a trumpet foghorn, which he wound, like Roland, into the western glow.

Time seemed to stand still, yet the hands of our watches passed eleven.

Barrow stood silent, gazing now into the west, now towards the jetty, where the sentry had paused in his beat, wondering what subversive activity could be connected with the braying of a horn. Torn between guilt and exasperation, we soothed Barrow, as our duty was, with assurances that if he explained the situation to the sentry on landing, all would be well. But the only effect of our efforts to relieve the tension was to induce Fiona to break into a disconsolate howl.

At last the dinghy approached. We all shouted at the occupants to hurry. But now they coyly hung off, calling that they knew what we were up to and that they had no intention of being soused again, as they had been before! It was eleven-thirty when Barrow embarked.

When I returned, after delivering him to the mercies of the military police, Margaret and John had disappeared. I found them in the engine room, collapsed against the clammy steel of the air bottles.

They were groaning, and their faces were twisted and streaked with tears, so that it was difficult to tell whether they laughed or wept.

13

NEVER A DULL MOMENT

"Who'll come a-waltzing. Metinda, with thee!"

EARLY IN July, John had received a message from the R.A.F. recruiting authorities to say that if he cared to renew his application he would probably be accepted. "Look here," he said, "I feel very bad about this as regards you two. But I'm not going to apologise. I had no idea of this when I joined you. The fact remains, I do know something about aeroplanes, and I think that Dunkirk is going to reverse a good many decisions that were made six months ago."

John had raced twice in the King's Cup. When he had volunteered for the R.A.F., he had been turned down because of slightly defective eyesight. Now, he was wanted. It seemed that we were fated to lose our partners just when we had become really fond of them and they had become part of the show. John's strength was his imperturbable humour. Only he, in the middle of a defensive explanation, could have removed with his handkerchief from Barrow's shoulder the effects of a high-level bombing attack by a seagull and assured Barrow gently that it was for luck! He never quarrelled with anyone unless they were either crooked or bad cooks; and he could convince even McCallum, who had worked in the East and was apt to be overbearing, that impatience was mere vanity and sad indifference to the essential jollity of the world.

Losing John Carr was a very bad blow.

Eventually, Margaret's brother, Richard, was able to

take his place, and to make sure, as John had always been
able to do, that we did not take ourselves too seriously.

Richard had sailed for years and was able to take a hand
with the *Mermaid* runs. And so it was that he became involved in the last ridiculous escapade of *Briarbank*—her
last revolt against the amateurs, which caused her summary
removal to Long Hope for the winter before Kenneth
Edmondson returned and made her behave herself.

We crossed in *Mermaid* on the 23rd of July, and again
on the 28th.

We found that *Briarbank* had acquired a neighbour. A
patrol vessel, called *Thelma*, nearly as long as herself, was
tied alongside her. This vessel was an ex-naval steam
harbour launch, converted to a motor yacht. She was com-
manded by her owner, an oil broker, rather deaf, who had
been given one ring and absorbed, complete with ship,
into the R.N.V.R. He asked us on board. He seemed a
pleasant, if slightly pompous, chap, and we warned him
tactfully about Baldry's exiguous mooring. Seeing a vessel
of *Briarbank*'s size attached to it, he had concluded that it
would hold another one. Moorings of any kind were scarce
in Ore Bay. The Navy reserved theirs jealously, and we
couldn't blame him for hooking on to *Briarbank*, though
we felt indignant and pressed our warning with vigour.

Richard, by this time, was enjoying himself thoroughly.
So far, the weather had been kind. Even an introduction
to *Briarbank*'s rigging, which we stripped with the aid of
a blowlamp and greased down, failed to damp his
enthusiasm.

On the 7th August we crossed again, this time with
nothing but bits and pieces for Barrow. There were
gelignite, detonators, safety fuse, electric cable, small pipes
and unions, paint, buckets, bolts, a coil of manilla, a coil of
wire rope, six parcels of rubber boots, oilskins, bedding,
two bags of oilcans, grease, tools, wire strops, spades, beds,
hampers, a case of whisky, and a violin. The total weight
was over six tons. Sleeping became quite a problem.

Briarbank had added to her train. Not only was the *Thelma* vessel still attached to her, but behind them both stretched a double tail of large, open motor boats. We learned, as we unloaded, that these had been requisitioned for ferrying work parties into some of the shallower landing places amongst the islands. What we could not find out at once was whom they belonged to. Presumably Jervis knew they were there. Since, in the matter of overloading the mooring, we had been the first offenders with *Briarbank*, and since we had still no alternative home for her, we felt that protests would be out of turn for the time being.

All the same, we were worried, as we tied up for the night on the outer side of her ugly old hull. If wind came, the mooring could hardly be expected to hold. We turned in in our clothes, with seaboots handy.

I woke suddenly in the middle of the night with the absolute certainty that something was about to happen.

Wind and movement registered themselves at once, but they did not seem too bad. The beam of a torch on my watch showed that it was three o'clock. I turned out with a sickish, empty feeling, dragged on an oilskin, and hove myself into the cockpit.

It was blowing a warm half-gale from the west, with soft dark clouds scudding under a bright moon. The sea was rising, but there was not much of it, considering the weight of wind. The warm air was less dense than that of winter and did not deal the seas so much of a blow. But our warps were under strain, and ahead I could see the foaming can buoy half submerged and the cable from *Briarbank*'s bow stretched to it hard and straight.

As I watched we began to move. I shouted down to the others, scrambled across *Briarbank*'s deck and yelled to *Thelma*, then back to *Mermaid* to start the engine.

"We'll have to get out," I told Richard. "There's nothing we can do to stop this. Stand by warps. As soon as we're clear we'll put the staysail on her."

The engine behaved itself. We shoved off and plunged

gently away to port, to watch what we fully expected would
be the destruction not only of our ship but also of about
five thousand pounds' worth of motor boats. There were
eight of them, tied four to a line, in two lines, one from
Briarbank's stern, one from *Thelma*'s, like a double string
of sausages.

Thelma showed no signs of having heard my hail, and
the whole outfit moved downwind past the wooden pier at
a steady pace. As far as we could see, the first thing they
would hit would be the Metal Industries' salvage trawler,
Metinda, which lay about a quarter of a mile astern. There
was absolutely nothing we could do about it. *Briarbank*'s
anchor was stowed; her cable and wire were both on the
buoy; and, in any case, we couldn't handle the anchor without the winch, which could never be started in this wind.
So we plunged about in the moonlit spray, and watched
for what was going to happen.

The cortège moved steadily down upon *Metinda*'s bows.
The motor boats were very near now. The end boat on our
side closed *Metinda*'s bows. Now it was past. It was moving
down her side, still afloat. The others followed.

We tacked and stood back; and when we looked again,
Briarbank lay alongside the forward half of *Metinda*'s
length, and the whole mass was plunging a little in the
larger seas of that place, but stationary.

We lowered sail, came cautiously alongside *Briarbank*,
and tied on a head warp, leaving the engine running. Then
we hoisted ourselves on to *Briarbank*'s deck and ran across
to see what the damage was.

It was darker now, but there was enough moon, assisted
by the beams of torches, to show that *Briarbank* lay snugly
enough alongside the big trawler and that apparently she
had not suffered a scratch. Her cable and wire led away for
ward with *Metinda*'s, which they crossed just above water
where we could dimly make out the can buoy in a welter
of spray, caught and canted against *Metinda*'s cable. From
it another set of gear led to the far side of *Metinda*, and

there, a moment afterwards, we discovered *Thelma*, complete with her string of motor boats, all intact and unharmed. The two lines had parted exactly at *Metinda's* cable and had draped themselves gently round her like a comforter. All eleven vessels were absolutely unhurt.

We were still comprehending this miracle when *Thelma's* skipper made a belated appearance in pyjamas and a duffel coat from his glasshouse amidships, and wanted to know what the —— —— was going on.

"You might have hailed me!" he bellowed reproachfully into my ear.

"I did," I yelled back.

"Didn't hear you!" He was strongly indignant with the world in general and the Almighty in particular, and wanted to know what he was going to do.

"Better go back to bed," I bawled, "before the Commander wakes up!" The *Metinda*, though owned by a civilian firm, was one of H.M. ships, and her captain, as we knew, was a commander, R.N. It could only be a matter of time before he woke up, or someone woke him up, and he took in the situation and went into action.

Thelma's skipper gave me an indignant look, and staggered back to his ship.

Having found a home once more after battling about at what had lately become for us a most unwonted hour, Margaret's reaction was to make some tea. *Mermaid* happened to be short of fresh water. There was none in *Briarbank*, but Margaret spotted a tap on *Metinda's* deck, outside the engine-room casing. Arrayed in duffel coat and bare feet, with her hair torn from its usual moorings by the wind, she was filling her kettle, when a man emerged from the fo'c'sle clad only in long woollen underwear. He saw her, rubbed his eyes, glanced wildly round at the invading fleet, and shot backwards into the darkness.

"That," I thought, "has torn it!"

We retired into *Mermaid* and made tea, pending the judgment. We were nearest to hand when the commander woke up, and no doubt we should get the benefit of his immediate reaction. We hoped that after that, if we played it properly, we might obtain his help. We should know more about that after we had met him.

It was Margaret who made the acquaintance. Either the man in the underpants had not believed what he had seen, or had considered that he could not appear before his commanding officer until he had dressed—and, in view of what that officer might have to say, had taken his time about dressing—but, whatever the reason, it was so long before anything happened that Margaret thought she might as well fill her kettle again.

The wind seemed to have strengthened during the past two hours. It had begun to veer and was piping up in furious rain squalls, as though it would reach a peak before dawn and then fall away with the day. Spray was dashing and spouting between the ships as they laboured together in the short but vicious seas, and rain lashed the decks and hid the setting moon behind dark driving curtains.

Margaret won across the heaving gunwales. It was not a time for caring about appearances. Being barefooted, ragged, and soaked was so common and necessary a condition of our job that she and anyone who knew her had long since ceased to think of it. But to an elderly commander such an appearance on the deck of his ship in a gale in Scapa Flow at five o'clock in the morning was naturally unsettling.

He looked at her for quite a time. Then he became aware of the mass of craft which surrounded his ship like an attack of pirates. He was still looking, when the whole mass, with *Metinda* in the middle, began to move downwind . . . !

Richard and I, watching from *Mermaid*'s cockpit, saw Margaret cross to *Metinda*, and a burly figure emerge from the aft companion with pyjama legs flapping beneath a black oilskin.

We saw him check, and stand for an appreciable time, as his eye lit on Margaret. Then he looked quickly to right and left overside. He had just—as we guessed—decided what he was going to say, when a sudden quietening in the turmoil of wind and water rang a fresh alarm, and we saw the dim shapes of buildings ashore sliding swiftly to our left.

Margaret vowed afterwards that she stayed long enough to give the commander a reassuring smile. But it seemed to us that in more like the twinkling of an eye she had slung her kettle into the cockpit, thrown off our head warp, and jumped aboard to take the tiller, as Richard ran the staysail up again and I cranked the engine.

As we crashed away, men began running on *Metinda*'s decks, and shreds of sound coming to us through the wind indicated that the commander had begun to express himself.

We never even met him, to thank him afterwards for sorting out the mess and putting *Briarbank* back next day on the big new mooring that Barrow had made for her. *Metinda* coped easily with the gale that night, for she always had steam up.

Instead, we met the King's Harbourmaster, in an interview from which humour was largely absent.

After spending what was left of the night in coy seclusion behind the *Greenwich*, we were hailed bright and early next morning by a drifter, with a message that K.H.M. wished to see the master of the *Mermaid* at once. The drifter took the master of the *Mermaid* off to A.C.O.S., to be received by Captain Frewen in the calm of a large office.

"I think we'll have to blow that ship of yours up," he began.

"Oh, please don't do that, sir," I managed to say. "She's a very good ship, really!"

"Ore Bay's getting rather crowded," he went on. "Not

much room, with all this new stuff coming up. Take her down to Long Hope."

I explained (1) that Barrow had now made for her an undraggable mooring, consisting of a block of concrete weighing a ton, plus another ton of inch-and-a-half chain, and (2) that *Briarbank*'s engine was under indefinite repair.

"Don't worry," said K.H.M., kindly. "We'll tow her down for you, mooring and all."

Since the night's frolic had carried away, amongst other things, two ship-to-shore telephone cables, and had immobilised the *Metinda*, a fleet salvage ship at instant notice, for about twelve hours, it could be said, all things considered, that K.H.M. was taking a generous view of the matter!

14

HARVESTER

"It was so old a ship—who knows—who knows?
—And yet so beautiful, I watched in vain
To see the mast burst open with a rose
And the whole deck put on its leaves again."

FLECKER: The Old Ships

I FELT sure that there was nothing seriously wrong with *Briarbank*'s engine. But it was plain—at last—that unless we bought an adequate compressor and found an engineer who was used to these large, rather temperamental, and rather dangerous semi-diesel machines, we could not run the ship.

So we had decided to try the *Harvester*. It would mean unknown expense; but, having seen her type, I looked forward to making her acquaintance with feelings of hope and relief. At least, she was made of wood, and still had sails!

I parked my bag in the hotel at Anstruther, and went by bus to St Monance to meet the Sandisons. Bob, the son, with whom I had corresponded, was doing ferry work in Scapa Flow, but the old people were at home, and in them I was privileged to meet for the first time two of the finest of a generation of fishing folk that has now disappeared as finally as the boats that bred them.

Mr Sandison, senior, was a tiny wisp of a man. I could not understand how he could have been physically capable of the work a big sailing Fifie involved. The leach of the mainsail measured ninety feet. The lower block of the tie purchase weighed a hundred pounds, and had to be passed across the deck every time the ship was put about.

Yet the sailing was the least of the work. Every night's fishing meant handling half a mile of nets four times—shoot; haul; overhaul for cleaning, mending, and drying; then flake down into the ship again, ready for the next night's work.

The hauling, by means of the heavy buoy warp, to which the nets were attached and the ship herself lay whilst drifting, had in those days to be done by hand. They would do it, night after night, in the full fetch of the Atlantic, twenty miles north of the Butt of Lewis, and be back to Stornoway before dawn to land the catch.

"Ships of wood, and men of iron" the saying was. Old Mr Sandison must have been made of steel wire. His sons were fine big men, twice his size, but they had grown up with Gardner engines and steam capstans. Work such as their father knew is not done nowadays.

He looked very hard at me out of fierce eyes from beneath brows like an Old Testament prophet's, and his jaws worked meditatively. I told him something about what we were trying to do in the north. I hoped—vainly, as I knew—to soften for him the blow of parting with his ship, by persuading him that she would be going to do a not-unworthy job. This was necessary, since the *Harvester* had been a second home to him and his family for forty years.

He went over her with me that morning from eyes to sternpost.

She was very silent, very tidy, and going aboard her was like going into another man's loved house.

The fo'c'sle, where the boiler stood, was a cavern of black wood, that was like a sanctuary, its great ribs and baulks centring in the tabernacle of the old mast. A piece of the original mast, eighteen inches through, had been cut off and left as a step for the new, which was a mere stick, fifty feet long by twelve inches thick at the butt; the tabernacle had been narrowed by cheeks of wood three inches thick, to take it.

The wide, scrubbed hold was like a pleasant loft, or

attic, where children might play, enchanted by the salty
smells and the deep niches between the ship's timbers. The
place was eighteen clear feet wide and eighteen long. The
sunlight slanted into it in dusty beams.

Only a board partition separated the hold from the
cabin. There was a square hole cut in this partition, closed
by a sliding hatch, for air and for verbal communication
when necessary, but there was no doorway. The hold was
for work; but the cabin was home: you reached it only
by a hatch abaft the skylight where the ship was narrowing
towards the stern, and went down into it, facing forward,
by a short flight of steps. It occupied the whole after end
of the ship, a vee-shaped space lined with eight bunks, like
cupboards, in two tiers each side. The sliding doors of the
lower bunks made backs to benches, which were also locker
lids and ran round on each side, with a triangular table
between them. Forward of the bunks on each side were
fuel tanks, shaped to the slope of the ship's sides. There
was a small coal range forward, on the right, set against
the partition.

And there were the engines. *Harvester* had two of them
—the big, black Gardner in the middle, and a 30-h.p.
Kelvin in the gloom forward on the port side.

It was laughable and it was charming to see how
obviously these engines were intruders of the younger
generation. They bulked so large, and yet they had not
been allowed to make the cabin look in the least like an
engine room. They were spotless, and yet there was no
sign or litter of their accessories. The new linoleum that
Mr Sandison—or Bob—had recently put on the floor for
the honour of the ship, was more obvious than they. They
had been an economic necessity, that was all. Bob and his
brother, David, loved them, of course; but the heart and
memory of old Mr Sandison were in the domestic arrangements of the place—the plates and cups that he produced
with shaking hands, and the little wooden knife-box that

Bob had made, filled with forks and spoons, bent but spot-
lessly clean.

He held them out to me, as though challenging me to
be worthy of them. It was part of himself that he was
sacrificing, yet it was also part of the ship's inventory, and
he had taken my money for it. Most of his sharp, creaking
Doric was indecipherable to my southron ear, but there
was no mistaking his own interpretation of his bargain:

"I've pit a' thing abaird. Ye see? Knifes, and speans,
and things fer mekkin' semmoliny, an' a'!"

During the two days that I spent in *Harvester*, measur-
ing, planning, and making notes of what had to be done,
old Mr Sandison was never far away. Attempts to hide with
a note-book in corners of the ship and to create a magnetic
field of privacy were no use at all. He would pursue, or
stand alongside on the quay, discussing the situation with
his friends, and now and then his disgusted murmur would
come down to me in hold or fo'c'sle or cabin: "He's aye
plannin', plannin'!"

There were three main alterations to make. The biggest
was bulwarks. Mr Richardson, the Board of Trade surveyor, insisted on that. I liked bulwarks, but a hundred
and sixty feet run of bulwark two feet four inches high,
with six by three stanchions every three feet, meant a lot
of timber. However, it had to be done. Next, the steam
capstan must be fitted with a reverse gear and brake, and
a boom must be found to take a load up to two tons;
the mast was a beautiful clean stick of pine and would do
as it was, but it would need heavy staying with long shroud
plates and steel wire rope. Finally, for convenience in
manœuvre, I wanted all engine controls brought to the
wheelhouse.

Of course, one could not just order these things. It took
a great deal of visiting, waiting, talk, and diplomacy to get
matters in train. As to time, the builder, who had the biggest job, finally admitted to a month. I reckoned this could

safely be doubled, even if personal pressure were well maintained.

Then, seizing this first available chance, Margaret and I went south for a holiday, leaving Richard and James Sinclair to work the *Mermaid*.

When we returned to Anstruther, the work was well under way. We spent a strenuous and expensive month finishing the refit and provisioning the ship. There was a raid, in which no one was hurt, but a coal shed behind the house belonging to our old friend Peter Stewart, the skipper of *Calliopsis* at Scrabster, was completely atomised, together with the three tons of coal it contained. The moon that night shone upon a quaint gathering in the garden of the hotel in various stages of night attire, lightly covered with coats and pullovers—the landlord, purposefully grasping a twelve-bore loaded with buckshot, the bank manager with a deer rifle, and Margaret and myself with *Harvester*'s strip Lewis propped against a pergola, which was still covered with late roses.

Richard and James and "Choorge" came down to take the ship to Scrabster. I could not risk going with them and possibly being held up, for news had come that Kenneth Edmundson was free again, and I was in a fever to get back and talk to him. Sandy Allen, a local man, who had acted as shipkeeper in our absence and knew Gardner engines, was engaged as engineer, and a youth, Eckie Duncan, as spare hand.

At Scrabster, the bush telegraph, that seems to operate upon sea coasts only as it does in jungles, reported that Barnwell's latest boat, the *Shannon*, had gone ashore on Westray in a north-west gale, having dragged no fewer than five anchors, and that, while mercifully no one had been lost, Kenneth was wearying of such performances. After protracted negotiation, he promised to come to us early in the new year.

A less fortunate piece of business was our failure in what we afterwards referred to as "the battle of the house". We

had agreed, with Norton's consent, to rent the half of a
cottage in the village. We arrived back in Scrabster to find
he had commandeered it. We were sore about this, for the
idea of living in *Mermaid*'s fo'c'sle through another winter
and sleeping on bags of bolts, when she was loaded, in conditions of gale, frost, and snow, had begun to lose its charm.

Richard later celebrated this event with an ode in the
Augustan manner. After describing the plaintiffs:

> "Two Wights there were, debased of mien and mind,
> Shabby before, inelegant behind;
> No gold they wore, no brazen buttons bright—
> Their hands impure, their collars far from white"

he devoted several stanzas to the history of the case, magni-
fying the characters to epic proportions, until he came to
the crisis:

> "As ireful Jove bends down his brows in wrath
> And with dread gesture calls the sinners forth,
> So noble Norton, Rhadamantine hand
> Thrust in his pocket, bids the couple stand
> Before his face to hear their doom pronounced,
> And, hearing, understand they had been bounced!"

This was hardly fair, perhaps, to Norton, who was in the
unenviable position of having to disappoint somebody; but
we felt rather strongly about the matter, and it cheered
us up.

We did a run in *Mermaid*, with a cargo of urgent bits
and pieces for Scapa and Lyness, visited *Briarbank* in Long
Hope, where we seemed to hear Kenneth's voice in her
dank engine room, saying cheerfully "She's *got* to go!"
and, seizing a chance in the breaking weather, crossed to
Scrabster in time to meet Richard.

He came in with *Harvester* on the 30th November, eight
days out from Anstruther. He had met no enemy, but a
great deal of rough weather, which had driven him back
to Fraserburgh and then held him with a full gale for three

days in the small awkward harbour of Portknockie. The
ship had behaved well, and the crew were all cheerful. I
felt that Richard had put up an extremely good show. It
was the first time he had ever handled a boat of *Harvester*'s
size, and he had brought her two hundred miles, mostly in
heavy seas, had used his judgment in turning back for
Fraserburgh before the wind reached gale force, and had
kept her clear of damage for three days of full gale in a
small exposed harbour.

McCallum and Barrow had a plethora of cargo waiting
for her, and she did three runs during December in fairly
rapid succession, sailing from Scrabster on the 9th, 16th,
and 22nd. The cargo was all contractor's stuff of the kind
and variety *Mermaid* had lately been carrying, but of
course in considerably greater bulk. She could take sixty
tons—and did on one occasion, when the load was topped
by a sectional hut, eighty feet by twenty, whose sections
filled the deck to the level of the wheelhouse windows.

I shipped in her for the first few trips, for I wanted to
see exactly how things would go and be on the spot to help,
if needed.

The main business, of course, was in harbour. We all
worked at full bore from the time the lorries started to
come down in the morning. With from twenty to thirty
lorry loads to put in, and darkness closing down soon
after four o'clock, loading was seldom completed in a day.
Sometimes the days passed in a sharp, crystalline stillness,
with a bright sun, warm at midday, so that James, stowing
in the hold with Richard, or Eckie Duncan, would strip
off his butcher's overalls, wipe the sweat from his mahogany
face, and crack jests with the lorry drivers. Sometimes the
quay was swept by a driving mass of rain or sleet mixed
with spray, in which oilskinned figures staggered and
cursed, while the tally man had to shelter in the hold to
keep his book dry.

A sailing morning made, as usual, a little peak of tension.
There was still the weather to guess at. And I could never

quite dismiss the engines from the debatable land until a cloud of white vapour and a ridiculous, homely, "tittup-a, tittup-a" from *Harvester*'s stern showed that Richard and Sandy had got the Gardner off; to be reinforced, a moment later, by the deeper thrumming of the Kelvin. Getting under way was a deliberate, stately operation, requiring warps and nice judgment to clear her projecting rudder from the wall and start her bow swinging at the right time.

Clear of the harbour, she seemed as light as a cork, yet as steady as a battleship. She gathered speed quite imperceptibly. Her lines were so clean that you had to go forward and look over the bulwarks to see her bow wave. On the second trip, as we were leaving Lyness, Bob Sandison spotted us and came after us in the little *Briar*, which we had first seen in Invergordon and which was now a ferry working in the Flow. She came with a bone in her teeth at what appeared to be a high speed, whilst *Harvester* seemed to be scarcely moving. Such was the comfortable effect of bulwarks and great beam, combined with an almost perfect form of hull.

Comfort in other directions was not altogether unmixed. It was luxury—childish, perhaps, but extreme—to steer from an enclosed wheelhouse or to be able to dry wet clothes at a coal fire. Yet, after a day's run, with the engines slowly cracking off their heat, the stove red for supper, and a vapour composed of paraffin, tobacco smoke, and carbon dioxide filling *Harvester*'s cabin, it seemed that the atmosphere could be cut into chunks and carried out on deck.

At bedtime, however, James, who had spent the day in a north-east wind at some degrees below freezing, would bank up the stove with slack, draw the hatch tight shut, pull his cap well over his ears as he turned in to his bunk, and settle down to sleep with a half sigh, half murmur, which sounded like "Ah yes, mon!" and showed he was satisfied that atmospheric conditions were about right for a good night's rest!

When I thought he was asleep I would get up quietly

and open the hatch a modest crack. I had been careful to choose one of the bunks at the after end, as near the hatch as possible, and in an eddy, composed of carbon monoxide going out and a faint dew-cool draught of oxygen seeping in, I would fall into unconsciousness.

Some time later, I would wake up with a strangling at the throat. The hatch would be shut. Below me there would be the scrape of a match, James's face illuminated for a moment beneath his cap, then the glow of a cigarette butt in the dark, and, after a while, a satisfied sigh of "Ah yes, mon", as he turned again to sleep, convinced that he had thwarted some ill-designing person, who would have given him his "death o' cold".

As a team, we got on well together. The only discordant note was struck by Eckie Duncan, a spoilt youth, who had been brought up by a doting grandmother. He dealt persistently in the three or four adjectives which become so wearisome to listen to after a time, favoured us with his opinions upon everything in heaven and earth, and refused to remove his hat even at meals.

"For what use are ye?" James said once, in his quick, low voice, his lip lifting in his great dark face. "Ye canna do ocht but sweer! Ye're aye sweerin'. If ye was to read yer bleddy Bible a bit more it'd be the better fer ye!" And he tittered suddenly, as he realised that his last remark might have been better put!

The quiet Sandy was rather a butt of young Eckie's, until one evening he, too, had his word to say, when he asked Eckie mildly why he didn't take his hat off when he came to the table.

"Why should I take ma hat off?" demanded Eckie truculently.

"Because, if ye hae nae respect for the company, ye micht hae some fer yeersel'," replied Sandy drily. He thought for a moment, and then added, with a ghost of a smile, "And shall I tell ye another reason? It's because if ye was to take yeer hat off sometimes, it'd mebbe gie yeer brains a chance tae expand!"

Christmas came, with perfect, still, cold weather, and a light snow on the ground.

Harvester's crew went home for a week's leave.

Thanks to presents of food, we were able to do proper honours to the day. A turkey was cooked in *Harvester*'s small oven, having been flattened by main force to make it go in. Margaret had made a cake, which she concealed successfully until the appropriate moment. Richard dressed *Harvester* with a holly bush at the masthead, a proceeding which upset and scandalised James—perhaps because it savoured of Popery. In the afternoon we worked off our dinner by snowballing, and by tobogganning on a home-made sledge down the brae. This also incurred James's displeasure when he heard of it; and he told us how Kennie, the engineer of the lifeboat, had hit the wall at that place and been never the same again.

During January the weather worsened. Gale followed gale, with scarcely a pause. In the hills by Forsinard the snow was falling, and the wind was piling it over the shedding on to the line. Traffic stopped, and word came that the snowploughs were out trying to force a way through the blocked cuttings.

We cleared what cargo Burns Chalmers had at Thurso and took it over on the 3rd, returning on the 7th with a cargo of empty oxygen bottles from Barrow—our first and almost our only return load.

After that, for days on end, the outlook at Scrabster was the same; steel-grey skies falling to the grey-white skylines of Dunnet and Claredon; black water, black stonework, and black tracks scoring the pocked white of roadways and quays; white slabs of roofs, and white pencillings where the snow caught and clung on the windward sides of things; the black hull of *Harvester* and the now rather off-white hull of *Mermaid* for ever rising, falling, and shifting, in the tormented swell.

Mermaid needed constant attention in this sort of weather. Since it was clear that her usefulness was temporarily at an end, we took her mast and her remaining ballast out with *Harvester*'s derrick, and she rode more easily.

The war was beginning to wear the same grim aspect as the weather. For six months, since the fall of France, Britain had been fighting alone. The daylight air battle had been won, but the night raids had not yet reached their peak. The attack by sea was in full swing. Ships were being torpedoed almost at the mouth of the Firth. The half of a great hull, its open end gaping like a bombed building, was towed into the Flow and beached at Lyness. Once, for a week, Thurso Bay was full of timber, great baulks twelve inches spare, which were unapproachable in the sea that was running.

Thankful that we were not on the northern patrol in this weather, we turned to the scarcely more pleasant job of sorting out our finances.

We had discovered that to make her expenses as a carrier, with payment only on tonnage delivered, *Harvester* must run very regularly, with full cargoes—a condition made absolutely necessary by the absence of any return cargoes from Orkney. We had thought, up to the time of fitting out, that this condition existed; but the present hold-up proved that it was not quite sound enough to be relied upon.

Harvester had cost £600. Her conversion had cost a further £600. Her ordinary running expenses came to £35 a week. This included wages, fuel, ship's gear and running expenses, and the very heavy insurance charged for explosives, winter work in the Firth, and third-party risks. It did not include depreciation, major repairs, or refits. The ship did five runs in all during December and January, carrying 220 tons of cargo and earning £320

against running costs of £280. The margin was too small.
A small motor coaster of even 200 tons deadweight would
have earned twice as much with very little extra expense.

It was clear that the only economic hope lay in a time
charter.

I believed that a special use could be found for both
Harvester and *Briarbank*, due to their unusual lifting gear.
No drifter or seine-net boat, unless they had been specially
converted, was equipped to lift more than a few hundredweight. *Harvester* could lift a ton; *Briarbank* could lift
three tons. If vessels of their size were too small for regular
runs, they might vary this by poking about amongst the
islands, dropping heavy cargo in places where larger craft
could not lie. I explained the situation to McCallum, and
he said he would forward my proposition to Scapa; but his
firm did not at this time respond to my offer.

Rumours of our upstart concern had gone forth to
powers beyond Thurso, and in the middle of December we
had received a letter from the Scottish Command super-
visor of N.A.A.F.I., asking for details of the ship. He said:
"I understand that a trip could be made twice or three
times a week," and asked that our reply should be made as
comprehensive as possible. I wrote out a statement which
I thought would have served as an intelligent shipper's
guide to *Harvester* and the Pentland Firth, blissfully un-
aware that it would have served a better purpose if it had
been used forthwith to ease the recurrent deficiencies in
Mrs Maclaren's lavatory. It received a courteous acknowledgment, and we heard no more about it for six weeks.
At the end of that time there began a train of action which
bore no imaginable relation to its contents: the first of
those major offensives we endured on the home front,
beside which the efforts of the enemy or the sea seemed
a relief. . . .

At last the railway was cleared, and pent-up cargo began
again to flow northwards. I sailed with *Harvester* on the

26th January. Richard had had his pipe driven into the roof of his mouth whilst climbing behind Margaret up the Jacob's ladder of a Polish destroyer in the heavy run outside the harbour, so for this trip he stayed behind.

During my absence, a Norwegian boat, the *Ripa*, came into Scrabster, full of refugees. All but two of her crew left for London at once. The skipper afterwards served with the organisation of boats and men then being built up in Shetland, which later maintained such constant contact with Norway that it became known as the Shetland Bus.

Before he left he had supper aboard *Mermaid*, and presented Margaret and Richard with all the remaining stores in *Ripa*. The operation of sorting them out and transporting them along the quay to *Mermaid*'s berth was one which they found entirely fascinating.

They were still at it when I got back with *Harvester*.

It was an inauspicious evening. For the first and only time, I was caught out in the Firth by really dangerous weather. Perhaps the size and comfort of *Harvester* and her general reliability had made me careless.

We had finished unloading at Scapa the day before and had come down to Lyness in the morning with a falling glass. However, at midday the sky was still quiet, and we asked for the Switha Gate and started out.

The gale fell on us from the north-west when we were half-way across. Fortunately we were clear of the Men of Mey, the race that runs from St Johns to Tor Ness, but we had still to go through the uncharted mess that streams out on the west-going tide from Dunnet across the mouth of Thurso Bay. When we reached it, the seas were shortening and steepening, and their tops were coming off. The big staysail started to split, and we had to take it and the mizzen off. After that, *Harvester* rolled and pitched unchecked.

It was weather that I would not have answered for in *Mermaid*; I believe too much water would have come into the cockpit, once she was in the race, since the seas there

were shockingly steep and confused. *Harvester* was thrown
now on her bows, now on her beam ends, her propellers
either racing or choking, but she still made good headway
with the quartering wind. She was so buoyant that she took
no really heavy water on deck.

At last we got out of it, into the lee of Holburn Head,
and worked into the harbour in pitch darkness and sheets
of rain at about six o'clock. We berthed astern of *Benduff*,
very wet and tired, with that hollow feeling inside which
comes of being also cold, frightened, and extremely hungry.
I renounced the warmth of *Harvester*'s cabin, and fought
along the streaming quay to the place where *Mermaid* lay,
strongly expectant of supper and an audience for an epic
tale of storm and peril.

Mermaid's cabin was dark and empty, save for a mass of
alien objects, which I presently identified as consisting
of rope, tins, and potatoes. I wondered what on earth was
happening.

There were shouts from the quay.

"Hallo, there. Coming down!" And an enormous crate
scraped down the wall at the end of a rope.

"What am I supposed to do with this?" I cried, my words
torn away by the wind.

"Unpack it, of course! Don't take the sling off. We've
another lot to fetch!"

They had another lot to fetch. Whether the cold eats
into the bone, the rain soaks, or the black night shrinks
the soul, depends, of course, upon one's interest in what
one is doing!

The next load added its streaming masses to the heap
in *Mermaid*'s cabin.

"We're out of water!" was the next announcement; and
I helped to battle with the water breaker two hundred
yards along the quay to the pump, and back again.

Then I listened to the story of the *Ripa*, while, for half
an hour, we stowed away her unappetising loot.

When at last supper had been made, and eaten, and cleared away, Richard broke the strained silence.

"This came for you today," he said, and pulled out of his pocket a fat envelope with O.H.M.S. in black type across the top. It contained a notice requisitioning *Harvester*, with a covering letter, which stated: "His Majesty's Government relies on the goodwill of yourselves, your staff, and agents in carrying out these instructions and preparing the ship for the King's Service, especially as regards clearing cargo, fuelling, storing, and manning."

15

FRENCH EXERCISES

Q. Have you the Pen of my Aunt?
A. No, but I can lend you a Wheelbarrow.

I WRITE down the following events exactly as they occurred. Perhaps these old files and logbooks should have been burnt long ago, but I have kept them, with the rest, for sentiment's sake.

The comment is, I admit, one-sided.

Obviously, there must be Systems. What is still beyond human understanding is how large numbers of ordinary, well-meaning, hard-working people, when they set out to create and administer a System, can produce the effect of a Mad Hatter's Tea Party. "Alice felt dreadfully puzzled. The Hatter's remark seemed to have no meaning in it, and yet it was certainly English. 'I don't quite understand,' she said, as politely as she could. 'The Dormouse is asleep again,' said the Hatter, and he poured a little hot tea upon its nose."

There is the same suspension of all ordinary rules of life, the same inconsequence, the same dream-like unreality. It is like a combination of an elementary French exercise with a modern political trial.

With what pride and delight we received the order to prepare *Harvester* for the King's Service I need hardly describe. Gone were any doubts about the work and expense we had been at, in converting her for cargo. Gone, too, we thought, were our financial worries; for the requisition order stated that "M.V. *Harvester*, being required for urgent Government Service, is hereby requisitioned on the

conditions of the enclosed Pro Forma Charter Party T.98."
"The enclosed Pro Forma Charter Party T.98" was a
straightforward draft contract between ourselves and the
Director of Sea Transport for the hire of the ship.

I have often wondered how many owners of small craft
received "Charter Party T.98".

The document lies in front of me. It was never completed and it was never signed. It was subsequently
described by the authorities who had issued it as "inappropriate" and as "merely a guide". It never in fact had
any legal significance whatever, and, in view of its subse-
quent description by the Ministry, I can only presume it
was never intended to have any. But, not unnaturally, we
took it at its face value.

It had nine quite simple clauses.

The first set out that the "Owners agree to let and the
Charterer agrees to hire . . .", etc., the period being left
blank. The second states that the Charterer agrees to pay
hire, the rate being left blank, one month's hire being pay-
able in advance. The third requires an inventory of stores.
The fourth enables the Charterer to alter fittings. The fifth
reserves to the Charterer complete control of the ship.
The sixth relates to the loss of the ship, and the seventh
to re-delivery. The eighth states specifically "All risks and
expense of ship and stores shall be borne by the Charterer
during the continuance of the ship's service under the
Charter Party." The ninth and last clause merely excludes
Members of Parliament from being parties to "this contract".

The wording throughout is that of an ordinary contract.
The short preamble begins "It is this day mutually agreed
between ...., Owners, and the Director of Sea
Transport, Charterer", and at the end are spaces for signature of the Owners and of the Director of Sea Transport.

Harvester, then, "is hereby requisitioned on the conditions of Charter Party T.98". Nothing, on paper, could be
clearer than that.

We felt it was fortunate that the ship was clear of cargo
when the order arrived. We notified McCallum and
Barrow, filled up with fuel, made sure that the ship's gear
and insurances were in order, and on the 3rd February
sent a wire to the Principal Officer of the Ministry at Leith
placing the ship at his disposal.

The crew list had altered slightly. Eckie Duncan had
been dispensed with, since he had finally proved himself
uninterested in ship work, and Sandy Allen had not been
well and had had to give up. Another St Monance man,
well used to Gardner and Kelvin engines, had come in
place of Sandy. Richard was skipper, James was mate, the
St Monance man engineer, George Sinclair, James's son,
was deck hand, and I put myself in temporarily as fifth
man, as and when required.

Kenneth Edmundson had at last come down from Westray and was working on *Briarbank* in Long Hope, so
during the first week of February I thought I could safely
go over and join him for a few days, leaving Richard to
make out *Harvester*'s inventory and stand by for further
orders.

I fondly imagined that *Harvester* was now off our list
of worries, but that to put *Briarbank* into commission
again and find work for her would still be a problem.

However, with Kenneth Edmundson on the scene and
a private firm to deal with, *Briarbank* took on new life.
Kenneth found a second-hand compressor in a garage in
Long Hope, and within two days it was bought, ferried
off, tied up to the bottles, and had produced a start.

The failure of the after-cylinder to fire was traced to a
wrong adjustment in the injector, and to wear in the
rubber flap valves admitting air to the crankcase. As soon
as I could get spares, Kenneth put the trouble right in a
day. He did the same for the winch engine.

I wrote to Burns Chalmers on the 4th, offering them the
ship. They replied at once. We took her to Lyness, where
Metal Industries made a permanent installation of the

compressor. B.C.'s agent inspected the ship. A charter agreement was made by a simple exchange of letters early in March.

Briarbank went back into action at the end of that month, and, with only one interval for refit, ran without stop or hitch for the next eighteen months. She was kept constantly busy, running sometimes to Scrabster, but mostly between the islands. Kenneth reported that on one occasion she took on board a pair of diesel locomotives, each weighing three tons. And apart from McCallum's peculiar temper, which was what one might call a constant and could therefore be reckoned with, there was never the slightest friction or difficulty between ourselves and the company. All dealings were exact, intelligible, prompt, and in accordance with the simple, straightforward terms of the charter.

Full of cheer at seeing *Briarbank*'s engines running again and having Kenneth in charge of them—this time permanently—I returned to Scrabster, expecting to find urgent Government stores pouring into *Harvester*.

However, nothing had happened so far. Richard reported no letters other than an acknowledgment of our telegram. He had made out in triplicate a most comprehensive list of stores on board, and this we forwarded to Leith on the 12th February.

Harvester's expenses during the fortnight since the take-over had amounted to about £60, and I began to feel a twinge of uneasiness over a paragraph in one of the documents which had been sent with Charter Party T.98.

This document was headed "Memorandum for the Guidance of Owners". Paragraph 3 was headed "Crew", and stated that "In cases where it may be desired to retain the men on their ordinary form of mercantile agreement Owners will be requested to continue to accept responsibility for the manning of the craft and for the payment of wages, victualling, and insurance of the crew as if the craft had remained in their own service. The cost of such wages, etc., will be refunded to the Owners . . ."

No such request had been made to us. The Charter Party had not been signed, and we had no protection, in the legal sense, for the sums we were paying out.

In sending the inventory, I therefore asked what period the boat was to be chartered for and whether we were to continue to pay her upkeep.

Nothing happened for another fortnight. No letter, message, or money was received.

McCallum and Barrow now had a month's cargo awaiting shipment. Some of it was in the sidings at Thurso, some they had lorried hopefully down to the quay. McCallum's army coat and saturnine face were to be seen with increasing frequency at Scrabster, where he would parade slowly up and down, casting sour glances at his piled cargo, at us, and at *Harvester*, lying empty at her warps; her crew, having long ago done all the ship work there was to do, standing aimlessly about her decks, waiting for an instant summons to "urgent Government service". We had explained the position to him till we were tired; he had seen the correspondence; and, while we sympathised with him and had begun to feel as bitterly as he did about being unable to ship his stuff, there was just nothing we could do about it.

The ship's costs were now £125. On the 26th February I telephoned to Leith. The Principal Officer was away, and no one in the office seemed to know anything about *Harvester*. So I wrote the same day, explaining that our capital was not unlimited and that unless something happened soon we should have no alternative but to lay the ship up and discharge the crew.

On the 5th March a letter dated the 26th February arrived from London, asking for a crew list, and saying that in future the crew would be paid by the Military Authorities direct. This meant nothing to us: it was the first we had heard of "Military Authorities" being concerned in the matter. I sent a crew list, the same day, together with a copy of the letter I had sent to Leith.

On the 6th March, Leith got around to replying to our letter of the 26th February. They merely stated, as if in surprise, that "it was understood you were running for the Admiralty when requisitioned. The fact that you are lying idle has been referred to Sea Transport Department, London." The writer added "As you are in Aberdeen subdistrict, it would save time if you sent accounts direct to Senior Surveyor there." Still no money, no counterpart of Charter Party T.98 for signature, no cargo and no answer to the questions in our letter of the 12th February. Evidently some as yet undisclosed branch of the Army was interested in *Harvester*—not an encouraging speculation, we thought, where boats were concerned.

On the 7th March a telegram from London said: "Please expedite reply my letter 26th February, giving details of crew. You should accept instructions as to disposal of vessel from O.C., R.A.S.C., Stromness."

This telegram threw only a glimmer of light on the scene. It confirmed that the Army now had an interest in the ship, and indicated that the unit in question might possibly be R.A.S.C., Stromness. By this time I was becoming less interested in who was to dispose of the ship than in who was to dispose of her rapidly-accumulating debts.

On the 5th March, a Mr Ford had appeared unannounced at Scrabster, representing the N.A.A.F.I., and had looked at the ship and spoken to James. As ill luck would have it, we were all away that morning, and Mr Ford departed before lunch. Apparently, he had merely inspected the ship, asked the crew for a few details of engines and cargo space, and departed.

On the strength of this visitation I wrote that evening to the N.A.A.F.I. at Edinburgh—the source of the original enquiry in December—asking if they could tell us anything. They wrote a kindly letter in reply, saying that "the ship was certainly not chartered by this Corporation", but that they had telephoned to A.D.S. & T., Scottish Command, who had promised to take "immediate action". We wrote at once to this officer, confirming the now extensive history of the ship's requisition and asking him, if it was his responsibility, to do something about it with the least possible delay.

About the middle of March, *Harvester*'s engineer departed without notice. James told me he had been growing increasingly bored with inaction, and had taken to lifting his elbow of an evening in Thurso rather more than was good for him. He thought he had gone south to join a fishing boat. James was by this time rather restive himself, for he was not a lazy man; but he and his son were not prepared to throw up their berths just yet, though I could scarcely have blamed them if they had.

At about this time, too, military bodies began to appear from Thurso. They all wore impeccable uniforms beneath buff camel-hair coats. Their functions were obscure—even, it appeared, to themselves. Ships, tides, times, and handling methods meant absolutely nothing to them, and our outfit, in which everyone spoke his mind, if he had anything to say, was not to their taste. One of them, wearing red tabs, a monocle, and glassy brown shoes, after gazing for a long time at *Harvester*, turned to me and enquired which was the stern and which the bow. I could only feel sorry he had been sent to a place and a job he evidently loathed.

With only one of them was it possible to talk business.

It appeared, at last, from what he said, that the ship was to carry stores for the R.A.S.C. from Scrabster to Stromness. More than that he could not tell me.

He produced a long movement order from Scottish Command, prescribing in minute, prolix detail, the marking of cargo and a return trip for *Harvester* twice weekly across the Firth on specific days, as though she were a five-hundred-ton ship.

I tried to persuade him that there existed in the Pentland Firth factors such as weather, sea, and tide, which might prevent even the *St Ola* from carrying out such a time-table; but it was clear that he had already pigeon-holed me as a difficult and disrespectful type.

In the magnificent Log Book No. A.B. 104 for War Department Vessels, which had been supplied to *Harvester*, there were spaces for entry each hour of miles travelled, hours actually under way, winds, force, courses, and state of weather, and a large blank page for entry by "Ratings i/c" of the actual number of hours worked daily by each member of the crew. For thirty-seven days Richard and James had religiously inscribed on these virgin sheets the two brief sentences "Lying in Scrabster awaiting instructions. ...... hours of ship work done." We thought it wise, until at least we knew where we stood, to enter for "ship work done" a generous number of hours.

At last, on the 11th March, there appears: "Hands employed getting ship ready for loading. Started to load 4 p.m. Finished 7.30 p.m." And, on the next page: 12th March. 9.0 a.m. Sailed from Scrabster for Stromness. 5 tons of general cargo. 2 p.m. Arrived Stromness. Discharged cargo."

I went acros with the ship, and took the chance of calling on the R.A.S.C. at Stromness. There, after long delay, I was granted an interview with an officer who professed entire ignorance of our affairs. He said he had been told only that *Harvester* was to run to Stromness with stores. With the correspondence I had brought I got inside his guard to the extent of a promise that he would take the matter up with Scottish Command, and at that, since he plainly knew no more, I had to leave it.

We brought the ship back to Scrabster on the 13th, and thereafter the log entries reverted to their former two sentences until the 26th, when a further cargo, this time of eighteen tons, was shipped to Stromness.

By this time our balance at the bank had run out.

Burns Chalmers still owed us some money for the January freights, and I had to make an assignment of this debt to the bank to cover our overdraft for *Harvester*'s expenses.

Expenses were also being incurred on *Briarbank*'s account. It was an enormous relief to have her running, but there was a good deal to pay before the charter money for her first month would become due.

The *Harvester* business was now becoming a nightmare.

If the T.98 had been signed, I should have known to some extent where I stood. I could at least have tried the bank with it as security for the sums we were paying out.

As it was, we were now in intermittent communication with:

> The Ministry of Shipping, London.
> The Ministry of Shipping, Leith.
> The Ministry of Shipping, Aberdeen.
> The N.A.A.F.I., Edinburgh.
> A.D.S. & T., Scottish Command.
> A.D.S. & T., War Office, London.
> No. 1 Water Transport Company, Stromness.

From none of these bodies did it seem possible to get either a plain answer as to what our position was, or any admission of liability for the expenses so far incurred.

I had been working hard on *Briarbank*'s affairs, travelling pretty constantly to and from Orkney, and expecting each time I got home to find some message, letter, or person, that would throw some light on the *Harvester* affair. It was becoming very plain that unless someone paid us some money soon, we should have to close down.

One day, at the very end of the month, there arrived a letter from the Ministry's Aberdeen office which nearly gave me an apoplexy. It was dated the 28th March, and it was stated to be in reply to our letter of the 12th February. It continued:

"1. The period for which *Harvester* will be required cannot be estimated at present.

2. *You need not be responsible for manning the craft* but we will be obliged if you *continue to be interested.* [My italics.] Payment of wages should be arranged by the Paymaster at the Base for which *Harvester* is working."

3. Rates of hire for small vessels have not yet been fixed."

The letter added at the foot that our account of expenses for the period February 3rd to 28th had been "submitted for payment".

I wondered whether it was time to blow up or not.

For five weeks the ship had been completely idle, held immobilised by a Government order at the most urgent period of the war, while cargo, which she could have carried, was piling up on the quay. In a total of seven weeks, she had been given two loads, one of five tons, one of eighteen tons. Carrying this total of twenty-three tons across the Firth had cost somebody—us, up to date—over £250.

I realised, of course, that *Harvester* was a very small ship in a very remote place, and that the Government was conducting a very large war; but my humour was becoming such that this aspect did not at the moment address itself to me as forcibly as perhaps it should. Somewhere in the dim recesses of quirkdom our file was no doubt perambulating from in-tray to out-tray, acquiring initials and inertia as it went. But in the meantime *Harvester* was doing nothing, and our own capacity for useful work was being rapidly dissolved by a mixture of bankruptcy and despair.

The circumstance which made me decide at this juncture to swallow my spittle was the news of John Carr's death.

His partner in Belfast wrote to us at the end of February, saying that the ship in which John had been travelling (to join the air training scheme in Canada) was missing, and that the Admiralty regretted he must be considered lost.

We had little time to mourn him. His going meant that

we settled now with more grimness than gladness, not only to our work, but to our obligation to save intact, if possible, the money that he had put into it.

My reply to Aberdeen was therefore moderate and careful, though I still pressed for information.

By the 9th of April, we were still without payment or coherent information of any kind whatever.

On that day, *Harvester* actually carried twenty-six tons of tinned milk to Stromness. She had done a trip on the 4th, so this made her fourth trip in nine weeks. Her debts now amounted to £283 for pay alone, at the new scale, and we had spent a further £50 on her insurance and fuel.

I had by now so lost faith in any kind of Government authority that I decided matters could be made no worse if I took the lid right off.

I thought of the *Pearl*, in Wick, an old Zulu, whose crew on the orders of the Ministry, had removed their capstan and boiler (a considerable job), replaced it, removed it again, and for the second time replaced it, losing their summer's fishing and at last having the boat thrown back on their hands without compensation. I thought of a fisher man friend of ours from Fraserburgh, whose five sons had volunteered for the R.N.V.R., and who had then taken his boat, a big seine-netter, round to the western sea-lochs until the requisitioning authorities had got tired of looking for him. And there were the two brothers who had stripped the engine of their boat and buried the pieces.

I thought of these men with sympathy. I knew the crew of *Pearl* slightly, and I later came to know the Fraserburgh man well. They were fine men. They were not cowardly nor unpatriotic, nor mean: fishermen, of all people seldom are. They all knew about "Charter Party T.98" and they knew that without a typewriter, plenty of carbon paper, and some business training, they would stand very little chance.

Assembling the various addresses, I got down to it. related the story from the beginning, dotting every "i" and crossing every "t", giving reference, date, and quotation for every point, slinging back at them, in minutest, certified detail, the bilge with which they had been inundating me for the past two months. I almost began again to enjoy myself—enjoyment being mingled, however, with a sense of sick futility and fury that my own countrymen could, in the middle of a war, compel even so insignificant a person as myself to such a dismal waste of mind and time.

But it worked!

I believe that, in this country, if you write out enough accurate facts, often enough, to a sufficient number of different departments, the desired synthesis and spark will eventually ensue.

On the 11th we received from Stromness a cheque for the full amount of wages paid to that date. And on the 14th here came a three-page letter from London, which at last admitted something, and at last gave some concrete information.

The tone was frostily indignant, but the writer deserved full marks for his admissions. In the following extracts from this letter, the italics are my own.

"In order," he said, "to avoid any further misunderstanding, it is *considered advisable* to answer the questions raised in your letter to the War Office.

"1. Who has chartered this ship? *The ship has not been chartered*', but compulsorily requisitioned by H.M. Government for War Office Service.

"2. What is the charter rate? Hire for the use of this craft will be paid in accordance with the Compensation (Defence) Act, 1939. If you have already submitted a first claim, you can rest assured that *it is in process of being dealt with*.

"3. Form T.98, the blank charter party to which you refer, is intended *merely as a guide* to the general terms on which your craft is taken up, *formal execution of a Charter Party* in the case of requisitioned vessels being *inappropriate*."

"It is known," the writer went on, "that your vessel was lying idle some five or six weeks, but a very good explanation of this has already been received from the Military Authorities."

So much for "Charter Party T.98".

It had stated, in its second paragraph, that a month' hire would be paid in advance. We had still to wait a fort night, i.e. three months from the requisition date, before we received a cheque for hire for the first month, at the provisional rate of £10 a month. This just paid deprecia tion, at ten per cent, on what the ship had cost us. They later raised it to £16 a month, a sum which went so far a to pay also the interest on the capital laid out.

In the latter half of April, the atmosphere lightene considerably.

Briarbank was running regularly, and had scooped u Burns Chalmers's cargo from the quay and ease McCallum's blood pressure—I had begun to have quite fellow-feeling for McCallum.

Harvester's affairs were at last in some sort of order, an between the two our bank balance gradually lifted out the red.

Harvester was now running quite briskly. Her cargo seldom exceeded twenty tons, but I had long ago cease worrying about that. In fact, when we received a telegra from Edinburgh on the 22nd—"When are you upliftin 20 tons lying at Thurso awaiting shipment for fourtee days?"—I was not sorry to find myself under the necessi of replying "Your wire of today—approach R.A.S.C Stromness", since we had been told in no uncertain term by that body that *Harvester* was now completely und their control.

There was a continual stream of small fire from th Stromness direction, in the form of typed slips, most handed to James.

They asked us, for instance, for an inventory *Harvester*'s stores. I suppose, if I had had any sense, would have replied, "Please refer to Ministry of Shipping, Leith, to whom three copies were sent 12th February," but, instead, I sat down and flogged the whole five pages out again for them.

However, when they wrote on the 18th May, complaining of a shortage of cooking utensils and saying that "these should have been on board the vessel at the time it was requisitioned, and it is the Owner's responsibility for supplying same to the crew when necessary", I could not forbear referring them to the inventory I had just re-typed for them, which listed seventy-five cooking and eating implements of various kinds, and quoting our old friend T.98 where it stated "all risks and expense of ship and stores shall be borne by the Charterer". If T.98 was a "guide", it was presumably a guide, in the beloved modern phrase, "for all".

They had not done with us yet.

At the end of May, the Gardner engine became difficult to start. The ship had been running, on and off, for six months, and her engines were therefore due for overhaul in any case. During the year before we took her over, she had been lying at St Monance, and the Sandisons had given the engines a short run from time to time to keep them in order. They had not been actually taken down since the beginning of the war.

"Will you kindly confirm to me," said a shocked R.A.S.C. spokesman, "that this engine has run for this long period without overhaul?"

I gave him the facts.

What then occurred behind the scenes I do not know. James was by this time acting as skipper of *Harvester*, while Richard, as the only person competent since the St Monance man's departure, was looking after the engines.

Great as his merits were, James was not the man to bear peaceably with a certain type of soldier. So the engine defit may have been just an excuse.

Certain it is that *Harvester* was returned to Scrabster

on the 7th May, lay there, still on "charter", ostensibly awaiting refit, until the 9th July, and was then returned from Government service. Compensation of £10 was paid to us in lieu of the overhaul of the engines.

During her five months' requisition, she had been idle for three and a half months, and had carried 237 tons of cargo at an actual running cost, excluding hire, refit interest, and depreciation, which cannot have been less than £700.

16

AN OLD MAN'S GAME

" 'Tis time to be off out o' thees yer," said Uncle Jake.
"The lop'll rise when the flid tide makes. You may know
everything there is to know about fishing, but," he added
grimly, "if yu don' know when to be off, 'twill all o' it be
no gude to ee some day!"

STEPHEN REYNOLDS: *A Poor Man's House*

FOUR MILES across the bay from Scrabster the cliffs of
Dunnet front the Atlantic in a big three-quarter
circle.

From Dwarwick Cove, tucked into the eastern arm of
Thurso Bay, right round to Brough, tucked as snugly into
the north-eastern hollow of the neck, the walls face from
south, through west and north, to east, in a curving buttress
six miles in the circuit and three hundred feet in height.

This arc of cliffs is nearly, if not quite, as exposed as the
west wall of Hoy. At its foot, the shelf of tumbled rocks
extends outwards beneath the sea for some hundreds of
yards; and there, where the unresting surges pound and
pulverise continually the drifting meats of the sea, so that
a rain of food sifts, like manna, through the tangles into
the sheltered crannies of the rocks, the lobsters crawl and
hang in countless thousands.

In peacetime, we were told, there were never less than
three lines of creels, one inside the other, from Dwarwick
to Brough. Mankind will destroy any natural resource for
immediate gain, and in spite of the poor pre-war price to
the fisherman, even this great nursery was being fished out.
But the lobster, although it takes seven years to reach
maturity, has several protections which other fish on the

commercial list have not. It spreads its population evenly
amongst rocks, each lobster to its own hole, so that it cannot
be swept up in masses like flat-fish or shoal-fish, but must
be caught one by one; and it flourishes best in those places
which are most exposed and most dangerous to any kind
of boat—particularly on a lee shore under big cliffs, where
it has, at the same time, shelter amongst fallen rocks, and
moving water to dislodge food.

The local fishermen called lobstering "an old man's
game". Why it was supposed to deserve this title I never
discovered, unless modern improvements in inshore boats
and methods had, of late years, attracted the young men to
the more profitable seining and drift-netting, and left only
the older men to continue the poorer trade.

Certainly, the lobsterman could make his own pace. He
could potter, like the brothers Lindsay at Scrabster, along
a mile of sheltered coast, using a dozen creels, and taking
enough fish to make a bare living. But if he were young
and ambitious, he could use a motor boat and fish sixty
creels off places like Dunnet and Tor Ness. With a sufficient boat he might even venture, as one young Thurso
man did, the fifty-mile journey to Sule Skerry, and either
lose his life, dodging from lee to lee on that awesome
ground, or return after a few days with his tanks full of
huge old lobsters.

In past years, lobster fishing was the apprenticeship of
many an extra-master. Captain Swanson told me that as a
boy he had once made £50 from a single week's fishing
along Tor Ness, with lobsters at a shilling each.

It was hard work, and dangerous work. From May to
July it paid to drop the creels almost between the tide
marks. Any increase in swell or sea might set them inshore
or lodge them amongst the rocks and tangles, and it was
then, when lifting the jammed creels only a few yards
from the point where the swells hollowed and gathered
speed, that man and boat teetered on the edge of destruction. A famous diver, who learnt his trade with Cox and

Danks and was afterwards called on to go down to the *Thetis*, came of a Thurso family that had lost three of its menfolk in this way on the rocks under Dunnet Head.

Soon after *Briarbank* followed *Harvester* into active commission, Richard and I found ourselves dragged out of them by demands from the shore.

It was not so much the volume of shore work, as the absolute necessity for someone to be always on the spot, that prevented even one of us from signing on permanently in the ships. Constant journeys were needed, either to Stromness or Lyness, and while one was away the other had to be at the base.

This left time on our hands, and considerably less money in our pockets. Wages had risen to the point where there was nothing for the owners and managers of *Briarbank* and *Harvester* unless they worked aboard.

Lobster fishing, however, seemed to be a reasonable spare-time means of making good this deficiency. It required no capital to speak of, and it could be done, on and off, from Scrabster.

We began in April with a dozen creels, which was all *Mermaid*'s dinghy would carry. The drill was, to drop them in the evening and haul them first thing in the morning. Dunnet was out of range, until we could find a motor boat, so, to begin with, we experimented along the low cliffs between the lighthouse and Holburn Head.

For Margaret and me the delight of working together again in close contact with the sea brought back our early days in *Mermaid*. Even to be rowing out of a silent harbour in the dawn of a summer day was a perfect antidote to typing inventories in quadruplicate!

On the outward journey we would be in a hurry of anticipation. The rower would back the dinghy into the geos—cautiously, if there was a run on the rocks—and the man in the stern would grab the float with a boathook and eagerly haul in the buoy-line over the transom, watching for the creel to come clear of the weed.

Sometimes one could see, as it came up, whether there was anything inside. But one could seldom be sure, until the creel splashed through the satin surface in a glittering shower of drops, and a gleam and a wet clatter against the netting announced that someone was at home. The lacing would be untied, and the creature gripped carefully behind its arms and held up for inspection, gleaming like a jewel.

There can be few things more beautiful than a lobster straight out of the sea. It is utterly clean and sharp-cut, like a cameo. The colours are indescribable; they vary from the deepest, glowing blue-black, through shades of sepia, orange, and ivory, to purest white at the claw edges.

After the excitement of the chase, we rowed home more slowly, the stern of the boat piled with empty creels, and perhaps a dozen lobsters in the basket. Appetite for breakfast was sharpening inside us, but the garden of sea and cliff through which we passed was too enchanting for haste.

By this time, the sun would be looking over Dunnet, white and warm, bathing the bay in light, which, in the south, would have been dense and blinding, but here, in the far north, was bright and luminous as crystal. The surface of the sea heaved and trembled slowly: as unbroken, and apparently as unbreakable, as though it were covered with oil.

Near at hand, in the shadow of the boat, the water seemed an airy medium, so pure that the light sank into it, through fields of brown and purple weed, until it was reflected clearly, twenty feet down, upon the shells lying on a shadowy floor of sand. The breathing of the swell made the weed masses writhe continually, until every square yard hinted at lobsters of monstrous size.

In point of fact, each little geo was soon fished out. After three or four lobsters had been taken from it, the creels would draw blank for several days until new arrivals came in from the deeper water.

From the tidemark the flat strata of black-red shale went

up in cliffs of broken ledges, which, from April to June, were full of nesting seabirds. At the corner of Holburn Head, a mile from Scrabster, where the coast turned sharply west, the cliff was a hundred feet high, sliced out by the winter seas into long, smooth ledges beneath over-hangs, tier upon tier, where shags and guillemots crowded together amid noise and dirt, as in a vast tenement.

The fulmars were more select. Nearer Scrabster the cliff sank to fifty feet or less, and here, in the shelter, the tufts of sea-pink and scurvy-grass crept down towards high-tide mark. Where a tuft overhung a nook of rock, forming a desirable residence, a pair of fulmars might be seen cuddling and kissing each other amongst the flowers, with the complacent superiority of a pair of escapees from sub-topia!

Soon, we were looking for a larger boat. For we heard that a one-legged man from Brough was fishing sixty creels round Dunnet with an ex-ship's lifeboat, fitted with a Kelvin engine, and taking sixty pounds' worth of lobsters a week.

After some advertising and considerable search, we came on a boat at Thurso, which filled the bill.

She was a little old apple-cheeked lady, battered but cared-for, and she made the perfect foreground for an artist's impression of Thurso River, as she lay on her bilge on the foreshore, showing her full, sweet Fifie lines, her covered engine-space, open hold, and short pole mast stepped right forward (since it carried a single lug sail) in a tabernacle built into the decked fore-end. She was twenty-one feet long and eight-feet-six-inches broad and would stow about fifty creels.

Her owner led us to his house, where the pieces of the engine, a little two-cylinder 6-h.p. Kelvin, each carefully oiled and wrapped in sacking, were stowed, as being only less precious than a wife, beneath his bed. The boat was sound and the engine obviously in good order, and after the appropriate hesitations we closed with him for £45, and became owners of the good ship *Diadem*, of 2.38 tons, gross *and* net, built in Stroma "about 1908".

The next thing was to scour the countryside for creels. We needed two fleets—at least a hundred—since one fleet might be lost overnight in a sudden change of weather.

Although half a million pounds' worth of shellfish are caught yearly off Scotland, the industry has apparently been too diffuse to justify machine production of creels. The fishermen in each district make their own, to suit local conditions, with whatever material lies most handy.

The wicker pots of the south country and the big, slatted, churn-shaped creels of France and Norway were unknown on this north coast.

The local creel was shaped like a loaf of bread. It had a floor of slats from sixteen to twenty inches long and fourteen inches wide, into which were secured the ends of two or three half-hoops of heavy fence wire or withs from old herring barrels.

The covering was of netting, slightly heavier than herring net, with two short "funnels" of netting let in from opposite sides. The inner end of each funnel was a five-inch ring of fence wire, strained by a couple of strings to the opposite side of the creel, and guarded by a straight piece of wire doubled round the top of the ring and opening inwards.

The two funnels were just so long that the ends passed each other. Between them, secured at top and bottom in the centre of the creel, was a doubled string with a little slide on it to hold the bait. The lobster had to get himself well and truly into the creel to reach the bait, and, once inside, the wire guard fell behind him and prevented his getting out.

Owing to the broken ground, it was seldom possible to use a string of creels attached at intervals to a single line. Each creel had to be fished separately with its own buoy line, ten fathoms long, with small lozenge-shaped corks bound to it at twelve-foot intervals to keep it floating clear of the weed, and a big cork at the end to float on the surface and act as marker. The lift of all these corks was considerable; and this lifting effect, combined with the drag of the furious tides, made it necessary to keep the creel small and the netting fine, and to weight it very heavily with a flat stone bound securely in the middle of the floor.

Then there was the vexed question of bait. To rely on fresh cod's heads from Thurso or fresh gurnet from the seine-net boats was too uncertain. So we bought a couple of boxes of herrings and salted them down in a barrel.

After that, we acquired a forty-gallon drum, fitted it with a tap and filled it with paraffin. With the idea of an occasional night "at the herring", we also wrote to Bob Sandison and bought from him half a dozen drift nets.

Having by this time spent the better part of a hundred pounds, we were ready to start! Already a file of bills, receipts, and copies of letters had begun to swell; and once again a venture had become a business.

Our attempts at drift-netting were not a success. But I am not sorry to have spent five or six nights in the bay, watching the line of cork floats where it curved across the moonpath and waiting hopefully for the disappearance which would tell of a shoal striking the nets which hung beneath.

We learnt not only the fun of the game, but also a little —a very little—of the work involved. To haul by hand even six wet nets, each a hundred feet long by twenty deep, was quite a job, and the effort would be doubled or trebled if there were any wind. A scatter of silver where herrings were sticking in it would keep the crew going in brisk expectancy, hoping for the solid, blinding sheen of a heavy strike; but we never met it. There would be a box or two of fish, and then blank, dripping blackness to the buoy. And next morning the heavy mass must all be hauled on to the quay, spread until dry, and then carefully re-stowed.

The movements of herring in a bay are unaccountable. That summer, several small Thurso boats were out night

after night, and where one boat would take five cran of
herrings—worth £50 at the ruling prices—the others
would have only a box apiece, or nothing.

Lobster fishing was a steadier, if less spectacular, occupation. Until we were acquainted with the engine, we
fished along the low Claredon shore beyond Thurso, where
the penalty for engine failures might be less severe. But
though we spent a night there, anchoring *Diadem* and
underrunning our creels with the dinghy, we found the
fishing poor.

There were compensations, as there always are. We
caught there the biggest lobster we ever took, a crusted
monster of seven pounds, whose "big toes" measured nine
inches long and four wide; they were so heavy that he
could scarcely lift them. A lobster out of the water has little
power in its claws—far less than a crab, which can crush
its neighbour's shell as though it were made of meringue,
or squash the grain of a boat's thwart as a man could not
do with a pair of pliers.

One night, at Claredon, we had a view of breaking waves
from that unique standpoint: close to, and end on. The
rock sloped up to the shore in wide, flat slides, perfectly
formed for gathering the swells and inducing them to
break. Running into these rocks at intervals were gaps, in
which the water was deep and quiet enough to anchor the
boat.

From this position, the view of each swell, as it lifted,
peaked, and broke, was extraordinary. The top thinned out
as it rose, and then darted forward like a striking snake,
only to fall at once by its own weight on to the hollow
onrushing breast beneath. At the moment when it struck
down, there was a wide clear space of air beneath it, and
one felt that if it had been a little more viscous it would
have rolled itself up like a pudding. The play of light,
where the moon turned the thinning sheet to spun glass
and the break to purest snow, kept the man, whose job it

was to stand by the boat, gazing at that endlessly-repeated masterpiece for hour upon hour.

Soon afterwards, we went to Dunnet, where we began frightened, and stayed frightened, all the time the boat was on that ground.

Evening there was not so bad, for one had only to coast along, keeping clear of outlying lumps, and drop the creels over the side. But the place was a cauldron. It could only be fished in the quietest weather, the rule being that no white must be visible from Scrabster. The shelf of fallen rock, six hundred yards wide, was open to the west, and even on the calmest summer day the swell would heave up on to it and begin to trip and break, well out from the cliffs, the moment the tide changed.

In early morning, which was the time for lifting creels, this whole area would be in shadow, and the three-hundred-foot cliffs, though not large, as cliffs go in that part of the world, were high enough to make it almost impossible to judge distance. We would be appalled to find where we had dropped the creels in full sunlight the evening before. We would crawl in, the sea heaving under us like a beast, until we seemed only a hundred yards from the dank masses at the foot, and then drop anchor and take to the dinghy, to find that we had still a quarter of a mile to row before we sighted the floats.

I think the most gruesome part of the business was the deafening noise. It seemed to fill heaven and earth, as the roar and tumult of the surf clanged back from the face of the cliff. The man at the oars kept the boat's head out, one eye on the target of the float, and one eye on the swells, after they had passed beneath the boat, to see how long they lasted between boat and shore without accelerating and developing streaks in their backs—the signs that they had begun to break.

Every now and then, the ninth or the eleventh would heave the dinghy higher than the rest, drop it amid streaks of foam, and charge in, breaking and roaring, just ahead, before the oarsman, pulling for dear life, could get back to the next. Sometimes a creel had to be abandoned, after a nice judgment between safety and suicide.

The fishing was good. The lobsters were small—not much more than a pound and a quarter—for the place had been so heavily worked before the war that they had not yet had time to recover; but there was seldom an empty creel.

When a line of white could be seen under Dunnet from Scrabster pier, it was time to turn westwards along the coast beyond Holburn Head.

Just round the corner, a big stack called the Clett had been isolated from the main cliff by the battering of cross-seas thrown up by the end of the Dunnet race and the ebb out of Thurso Bay. Beyond it, the cliffs continued for two and a half miles, at considerably less height than Dunnet, but very smooth and sheer. There was no shelf at their foot, since the sea's assault against them was oblique rather than direct. Instead, it scooped out long ledges and slots, and where these lay between the tidemarks the surf would occult them with a deep boom and an eruption of compressed air and spray, which induced Margaret and Richard to christen them "flonk-holes". Except round the Clett itself, we did no good along these cliffs, until we took Geordie Lindsay along with us, for we did not know, as he did, where the submerged ledges lay.

When alone, we usually pressed on for another couple of miles to a low shore of bluffs and visible outrunners, protected from the west by a long, distant reef, called the Riff of Brims. It was a longish haul to Brims, but the fishing was good. The creels went down into deep vee-shaped valleys between out-jutting reefs, where there was reasonable protection from the mile-long whaleback of the Riff itself.

One quiet evening, we had put down fifty creels there.

The night was utterly calm, and the morning dawned as warm and bright as it had for the past six weeks. We thought there was even a slight heat haze and mugginess in the air—a rare exception to its usual crystal quality.

We pushed off early in *Diadem*, towing the dinghy, and as soon as we were clear of the harbour we noticed a considerable to-do of surf along the rocks. The sea through which we were running seemed quite quiet, as it did in the bay.

When we had gone half a mile, the west side of Hoy opened out from Holburn Head, showing a space of clear horizon between. This limit of sea, instead of being flat, was corrugated with vast undulations, which moved against the sky like a sea serpent. Presently, a dull, confused noise began to fill the sunlit air, and we could see that the Head itself was half hidden intermittently in a white upheaval. *Diadem* began to lift and fall at long intervals.

We looked again at the barometer, and scanned sky and sea intently, trying to discover what all this was about. Stories of rare tidal waves and earthquakes went through our minds. We knew that almost anything could happen in this part of the world, and so we crept on, dead slow, at the stretch of apprehension.

As we approached the Head, still in relatively sheltered water, we could see that an enormous swell was running steadily past it from the west. The weather showed not the smallest sign of change, either past or approaching. We examined the sea ahead for any hint of a break; for there was still a drain of ebb tide; but the summits were as oily smooth as the hollows. So, in considerable trepidation, we motored out into it, keeping well clear of the Head.

In a matter of a quarter of a mile, we found ourselves in a phantasmagoric world.

The warm sunshine shone from a white sky upon a scene which can have been rarely equalled save in the latitudes of Cape Horn.

We found ourselves in by far the largest swell any of us had ever seen. It is impossible to judge height accurately from a small boat. *Diadem* seemed to take a long time to slide down the mountainsides and trickle slowly up the slopes; and when she was in the trough the advancing mass hid everything, even the nearby cliffs. We were satisfied now that it was the aftermath of some fearful weather disturbance far out in the Atlantic. To seaward, the surface of the moving water was perfectly calm; a dinghy would have been safe in it. But as we rose upon the summits and opened out the line of cliffs extending towards Brims, we could only gasp at the sight.

The whole three-mile length was one raving mass of surf. Surf is hardly the word. Tens of thousands of tons of water were being flung momently a hundred, two hundred, feet up the cliff wall. So intense and continuous was the attack that it was difficult to pinpoint individual bursts. The great ridges of the sea were running slantwise to the rock, so that the cataracts from the upflung flank of one had scarcely fallen back before the next met them in indescribable confusion. Only where a fault in the rock made an out-jutting corner could one distinguish separate spouts soaring above the general smother, whitening the cliff to its very top.

A pall of mist hung along the wall, in which the sun presently made rainbows; and from the contending forces there beat an even roar—not deep-drumming, like a machine or a waterfall, but at once loud, harsh, and penetrating: a mass of sound that seemed to subsist not only in the air but in the very fabric of the boat, and in one's mind, dwarfing and submerging thought.

Through this glory we slowly ground our way towards the place where we had left our creels. The only danger we had to look out for was the backwash from the cliffs— what one of Hakluyt's voyagers delightfully called "the countersuffe of the sea"—which threw out breaking cross seas along the swell for half a mile; but we had only to keep far enough off to be clear of them.

In the little bay we found tumult enough. Had the main swell been on it, we could not, of course, have come near

But the Riff of Brims, a mile further west, was taking the main onslaught. Its half-tide slopes ran out directly in the path of the swells, and gave lee enough to anchor. Then we spent an exhilarating morning salving what was left of the creels.

Some had disappeared, the lines and floats dragged under and buried beneath the weed. Some, that had lodged, we had to leave, since to follow the buoy-line to where it led would have meant smashing the dinghy on rocks that came awash in the hollows of the swells. Eventually we saved about half of them, all more or less battered and with the baits untouched. But the loss was lightened by the intense excitement of handling the dinghy in a high confusion of sea, where an open bay and bright sunshine enabled everything to be seen and gauged.

The journey alone was worth it all.

Working home, as a little merchantman might creep past a naval battle, we were unable to take our eyes for long from the tremendous warfare on our right; save for a glance astern now and then, where the colossal burst on Brims hung in sight against the sky for a long time: a white portent, that slowly formed and as slowly disappeared, like the superstructure of a spectral liner.

17

" HOUSES AND LAND "

"Charm'd magic casements, opening on the foam
Of perilous seas, in faery lands forlorn."

IF TWO or three people combined to spend their summers lobster fishing and doing little else, they might find it a delightful and rewarding occupation.

It would bring them, in the finest weather (since it cannot be carried on at all in bad), to the wildest, most beautiful places.

If their gear were well thought out, with winches, tanks, collapsible creels, and so forth—things we had neither time nor money to obtain—they might take their steady £40 or £50 each week, during the six summer months, instead of the £15 or £20 which was the best we could do. And, being free of other cares, the background of heavy physical work would not be too much for them.

All these primitive occupations involve physical exertion, more or less, according to the pace. The sketches in the last chapter show only the pleasures of the game. It would be as wearisome to recount, as it sometimes was to endure, the hours spent in unloading the creels from the boat (half-a-ton of them), disentangling and recoiling buoy lines, mending, re-baiting, and re-stowing creels, maintaining boat and engine, and weighing, packing, and dispatching the lobsters and crabs to market. The runs out and home provided the only idle time, when the crew might chat, or speculate, or philosophise, or sing songs, or watch the gull that rode on the pile of creels in the dinghy, eyeing the bait inside and craning his neck from side-to-side in ridiculous indecision.

We enjoyed it greatly, but could have wished it had not been merely one of the things we had to attend to that summer. *Briarbank* was running steadily, but her paper-work needed fairly frequent attention. *Harvester*'s affairs, a kind of fantasy in quadruplicate, were like a perpetual toothache. *Mermaid*, though she was now floating light, as a house-boat, without mast or ballast, was still both a boat and a home, with the demands of each. And we had topped the load by hacking a garden out of the wiry turf of the brae, which had a slope of one in three, and building a house.

Housing was desperately short. If we wanted a house it seemed that we should have to build one ourselves. Another winter in *Mermaid* was to be avoided, if our exertions and finances could do so.

Advertisements and enquiry discovered a stout wooden hut in a field beside the Wick road some miles beyond Thurso. It had been built as a clubhouse for a golf course which had never materialised, and was constructed of very heavy board, over an inch thick. We bought it for £40. A Thurso timber merchant, who had a few power-driven machines, dismantled it and rebuilt it at Scrabster to our design. He was able to split most of the boards into two, so that with a little extra wood the material ran to a building thirty-two feet by eighteen feet. We approached Mr Miller, at Scrabster House, for permission to put it up on a clear space of grass opposite the Post Office on the quay side of the road. The framework went up in June and the inside work was not finished until September; but the furniture was in and we were installed before the bad weather broke.

Making allowance—as one can at this distance—for the novel delight of owning our own roof, I can say that the comfort of that little place was extraordinary: far beyond anything we had thought possible from such simple materials. The outside was simply of boards covered with felt, the sides painted and the roof tarred. Inside, the frames and collar-braces were lined with Gyptex.

We made four rooms under the main twelve-foot span of the roof—kitchen, living-room, bedroom, and office, each with its own windows in front (living-room and office had two windows apiece!), and its own door at the back in a partition running the length of the house. Behind the partition, under a lean-to extension of the main roof, ran a passage six feet wide; half the width of this passage was devoted to racks built all along the back wall, so that we could stow there, in warmth and dryness, all the spare gear with which we were burdened.

A large stove with a flat top and an oven had gone with the original hut. This we installed in the living-room, with its flue pipe going straight up through an iron plate in the ceiling, so that the fire was given a good draught and most of its heat was dissipated into the room.

I had long been convinced that a house in this climate should have certain characteristics. It should be built lengthwise and should face south, so that the rooms in which the inhabitants spent their time—that is to say, rooms other than store rooms—should each have a window facing the sun. Again, it seemed to me that the sole purpose of dividing a house into rooms is separation; and, if that were so, the separation should be as complete as possible, so that, for instance, the smell of cooking should not penetrate to the office, and the din of a typewriter should not annoy the cook! For warmth, all walls should have a double covering with an air space between, and as many walls as possible should be inside walls.

I thoroughly enjoyed applying these principles to our house and finding that they were justified, even on such a minute scale. The stove, of course, should not be allowed to emit gouts of smoke every time the lid was taken off for refuelling, and the floorboards should be tongued and grooved, like the walls, to prevent gales lifting the carpet but even in the best Council houses designers sometime go wrong over matters of this kind.

If plumbing and electricity had been available, the comfort might have destroyed us. As it was, the evenings spent, as the days drew in, with a good supper inside and a soft light from the Aladdin lamp shining on the cream-washed walls, made us increasingly reluctant to go outside and wrestle with *Mermaid*'s warps.

There was no room near the house for a garden: no room, for that matter, anywhere in Scrabster, except in the gullies of the brae at the back.

One of these gullies, behind a ruined cottage, afforded half an acre of scoop-shaped ground, sheltered from every wind but east. It was tilted at a fearsome angle and was covered with long, tufted grass.

There was no means of bringing manure on to it: the only access was a flight of narrow broken steps beside the cottage. But the soil beneath the turf was deep and good, for it was all topsoil, which had been washed down from above.

Working in relays, we trenched it all, breaking up and burying the tough hummocks. The earth worked down sweetly into a fine tilth, nearly free of stones. That first year of cultivation, everything was of show quality.

Just as war drives people to marry and produce a crop of sons, so it intensifies the curious satisfaction of growing things in the soil, despite untold labour. We even embarked on a hive of bees, but here our lack of skill went against us. They yielded a few pounds of the delicious dark heather honey; but we did not understand how to handle them, and in the autumn they deserted.

These domestic occupations, by which we sustained and consolidated ourselves in the intervals of attending to our proper work, were enlivened, one night in July, by a very close reminder of the war.

A new patrol trawler, the *Beech*, had replaced our old friend, the *Cape Portland*.

On Saturday nights the *Beech* came into the bay, and, in fine weather, anchored just outside the south quay, while her crew came ashore to stretch their legs and have a drink or two. We had heard that an enemy bomber had been seen in the neighbourhood during the past week. Many people seemed to know this; but the attack, when it came, was delivered in a flash and with a judgment that seemed to show it had been well worked out.

The first we knew of it was an enormous crash in the night, which brought us out of sleep and on deck in quick time.

Nothing stirred in the moonlight along the line of blank house-fronts, or in the quiet water, or the berthed ships. It was near low tide, and *Mermaid* lay well below the wall, behind *Benduff's* berth.

We shinned up on to the quay and looked over the bay. A trawler convoy happened to be there that night, and silence seemed to reign among the anchored ships. From the direction of Dunnet the faint sound of a retreating air-craft lingered in the air. . . .

Next day, we could see the top of a mast above the water, and learned that the *Beech* had been hit, and, with her whole side blown out, had sunk inside a minute, taking her crew with her. The German had swung inland and attacked at nought feet from behind the brae, with his lights on, dropping his bombs as he swept over the anchored ships, and escaping low over the water. He had probably not been within range of anything at Scrabster or in the ships for more than fifteen seconds.

We sat up for two nights afterwards nursing *Harvester's* Lewis gun, in a thoroughly dangerous frame of mind, for we were ready to empty it at anything that stirred. But of course we might just as well have stayed in bed.

From July to October this year, with *Harvester* out of action, *Briarbank* running in Orkney under Burns Chalmers's direction, and much to do on the spot, we were rarely away from Scrabster for more than a couple of days at a time.

Possessions began to accumulate. There was the half-finished house, the garden, *Diadem* with her creels and nets, and a considerable litter of barrels, drums, boxes, and suchlike. Richard was making himself some trout rods out of old greenheart baulks from the harbour. *Mermaid* was strung with drying fish caught on the way to and from the lobster grounds. And for a time—perhaps too long a time—there was the two-hundred-pound porpoise, which McBey, the foreman of the salmon stake-nets, presented to us, and which had to be flensed and rendered down for its oil, to supplement the dwindling ration of lard. The meat was good—like dark, tender beef—and the oil was clear, if pungent!

Our old friend, the skipper of the *Benduff*, shook his head over us. "Ye'll be getting rich," he mused, "in spite of all. Ships, an' houses, an' land! In yeer ain bed ivery night an' yeer wife aside ye—man, ye lack fer nothin'!"

This kindly, canny man was greatly concerned about our affairs. Margaret's presence bothered him for a long time; but when he accepted her it was with the regard and kindness of a father.

It did not take him very long to penetrate my business deficiencies. I was always blotting my copybook in his estimation, particularly in my dealings with James, whom he regarded as an undisciplined menace to our financial welfare. "Ye've got to be strict wi' crews!" he would say, with meaning; and, in spite of his small round form and comfortable face, he certainly kept *Benduff*'s crew in considerable awe.

One day, I upset him badly.

A boat from a Faeroese fish carrier came in, looking for a towing warp. The older of *Briarbank*'s two warps happened to be ashore; parts of it had gone black and greasy with mould, and its soundness was more than doubtful. So I let them have it for a couple of pounds.

When they had gone, Skipper "Benduff", who had

observed the transaction from afar and instantly understood the implications, came along in some envy and
curiosity to see how I had profited by the situation. When
I told him, I thought he would have a seizure. It was the
only time I saw him really upset.

"Two powun'!" he spluttered, and his voice rose to a
treble as he shot the words out again: "*Two powun'!*
Maircy on us! Man, I would ha' askit them *twenty* powun'
—*fufty* powun'! And I would ha' got it! Why didn't ye
let *me* speak for ye? Those men has *plenty* monney! They
couldna' find another ropie this side o' Wick—Inverness,
maybe. Eh, man, ye had them in yeer hand! Two powun'!"

I never quite lived this incident down!

As soon as the house was finished and our furniture from
the south brought up and installed, we were able to make
some return for all the hospitality we had received.

There was a marvellous diversity of visitors.

Skipper "Benduff" came in time for the last trout of the
season, which he pronounced "varra tasty". McAlister, an
engineer from Orkney, came half an hour early and caught
me having a bath in our largest washtub in front of the
stove. He told us how he had spent his life looking for a
stand of Kauri pine in the islands of the Pacific, and had
found it—on the eve of the war. Myers, a lieutenant in the
Scrabster Naval Control, who hated both the war and the
place, admitted that he had sold his fruit farm in Natal for
a third of its cost in order to come and join up.

Then there was the R.N.R. lieutenant-commander, who
had shared in the fantastic story of the *Arctic Queen* and
the *Arctic Prince*—two converted liners, which had been
sent by a Grimsby firm to catch halibut in the Davis Strait,
and had caught there an average of £1,000 worth of fish a
day for eleven years. The first of the fish weighed two to
three hundred pounds each and were probably a hundred
years old.

Skipper McMaster—he who had once smoked cigarettes
amongst the gelignite—looked in to bring us a "fry o' fish",

and explained, in answer to our unspoken question as to his long absence, that he had been for a few months in the Navy, but that he had "had a disagreement wi' a mannie, an' juist floated off!"

There were friends from Scrabster House and Thurso Castle. There were Captain Shearer and his wife—it was only from Mrs Shearer that we learnt how he had won a D.S.C. in the first war by sinking a submarine from his armed merchant ship. There were Ned McBey, the salmon fisher, and Mrs McBey, from whom we learnt something of what it meant to raise a family as the wife of an east-coast fisherman, and to dig bait on the beaches in winter dawns—all told with a richness of laughter and fun. Goodness shone out of those two.

Naturally, most of our friends had to do with the sea; and the bulk of them—as being interested in craft of similar size to ours—were fishermen.

Fishing seemed to endow men with the courage and endurance related of their forebears in the sagas. In our little *Diadem* we had barely touched the fringes of the easier forms of inshore fishing. With great-lines, the arduous winter standby of the local small craft, we had not even experimented and used to wonder, as we watched the *Children's Friend* from Thurso (reinstated by the war in her proper trade) unloading her hideous cargo of conger and skate and ling in the windy dawn, how we should have stood up to her night's work.

The boxes half filled the lorry, where the man receiving them unconcernedly thrust back into their unlidded tops a grey belly or a bloodied head, writhing clear of the slimy masses in blind, pathetic reflex of life.

To catch that monstrous half ton, two thousand four-inch hooks had each been baited and shot upon a total of two miles of line, and the whole hauled in again and coiled down clear in the baskets, the hooks twisted out of the fish and set into the rope grommet round the basket's rim. Once, whilst baiting and shooting at full speed, a hook caught the thick of the baitsman's thumb, and the weight of the boat sank it into flesh and bone deep over the barb. Rather than lose the night's work, he cut it out on the spot with knife and pliers and carried on.

Toughest of all were the crews of the Iceland trawlers. These men were not only the front rank of the fishermen, working in freezing ocean seas, six hundred miles from home, in the older and smaller of the North Sea ships (since the largest had been commandeered): they were also in the front line of the war, for they were under constant air attack.

Their trips lasted from a fortnight to three weeks. During that time each man might, if he were lucky, sleep four hours in every twenty-four. The ships would gather in the bay for their routing orders, bows flaring but hulls so laden with coal and salt that the side decks abreast the engine-room casing were no more than a foot above the water. They would return, laden as deeply with fish, and the crews would gaze listlessly over the bulwarks from black-socketed eyes in faces the colour of ash.

The strain upon the skippers was very great, even in peacetime. Like their work, they were big and they were tough. The older men would come ashore dressed in long white fearnought smocks, fearnought trousers covered to the knee by thick snow-white woollen stockings, black silver-buckled shoes, and—bowler hats! It was a strange symposium, at once fantastic, piratical, and faintly Biblical, with a superadded aura of conscious pride and power.

When we had first met one of them, a year before, he had invited us aboard his ship and given us eleven glasses of Benedictine before lunch. Lunch consisted of roast beef and Yorkshire pudding, followed by jam roll—all excellent and in large quantity. Then he had suggested adjourning to Mother Mackay's for a few beers, and seemed disappointed when we dumbly shook our heads and staggered back to our boat.

Two of them sometimes came off to spend an evening

with us. Always they brought a bottle of rum apiece, which they would plant firmly upon the table beside the one we had put there already.

Tom, who earned £1,500 a year, even before the war, used to spend his holidays at Monte Carlo: to him it was just a better Blackpool.

Arthur had lost an eye in a gale off Bear Island. "I was oop there, that time," said Tom. "It were a sea, worn't it, Arthur?"

"Ah," said Arthur, "it were a sea, an' all. 'Bruk wheel-'ouse winder." And that was all that they considered it necessary to say on that subject.

We thought Tom looked more worn and tired than when we had first met him. He spoke of his son, for whom he was buying an expensive education. He was bashfully proud of what he considered were the lad's brightest attainments:

"Thaugh Ah say it abaht me awn sunn, 'e is quick. Y' knaw, 'e works 'ard at 'is books. 'E's only fourteen, an' 'e knaws more at 'is age than what I do naow."

I thought "Does he?" but merely said: "And what's he going to do—go to sea?"

"Naw, Ah dawn't want 'im t' gaw t' sea."

"Does he want to?"

"Oh, yus. He's keen enough to gaw. 'E's been with me two trips—in the summer, like—an' 'e en-joyed it. But 'tis too 'ard. 'E shall 'ave better than I've 'ad. Naw," he finished, grimly, "Ah dawn't want 'im to gaw to sea."

The food and drink aboard these ships was always good, and now they have bathrooms and proper living quarters. But there is no short cut when it comes to handling the trawl and cleaning fish and working the ship off places like Bear Island. One can only hope that the sons of men like Tom and Arthur sometimes refuse to take their fathers' advice!

After *Harvester* had been thrown back on our hands I

tried to find some profitable work for her, but without success. She was too small to run with part cargoes, and, with *Briarbank* working to capacity for Burns Chalmers, there were no takers for a time charter. We had not the capital to put her back to fishing. So we sold her, minus her mast and derrick, which were to go into *Briarbank* to replace that vessel's rather shaky gear.

Parting with *Harvester* was for me a sad business. I had an affection for her which I never felt for the hideous—though perhaps more efficient—*Briarbank*. She was a very sea-kindly, comfortable, and safe old craft; and I am glad and proud to have sailed in, and owned, one of the last of her kind. When her broad lines and the white scut of her exhaust had dwindled for the last time across the bay, I had a feeling that for us, too, the time when we could be useful in this place was drawing to an end.

Briarbank was now due for refit. Besides an overhaul of the main engine, there were some alterations that had to be made—replacing mast and derrick, fitting a new winch engine, and converting the afterhold into proper quarters for the crew. I went with her to Buckie in November through a day and a night of thick fog—an alarming journey, in which Kenneth's idea of safe navigation was to "keep a grip o' the land". He had been that way so many times before that I let him alone, and in due course he identified Noss Head by means of the chute of ashes down the cliff beneath the lighthouse: this made him quite happy!

Briarbank's absence coincided with a renewed demand for explosives. Trade in gelignite had been slack for nearly a year, whilst the cementation of some of the underground reservoirs had been in progress. Now, some more blasting was to be done.

There was nothing for it but to fit out *Mermaid* again.

Once more Bill Harcus's handcart was borrowed to shift the mast and the loads of sails and gear to the quayside. As the days passed, and everything was checked, detail by detail, and put into place, we began to forget the labour as the old *Mermaid* became a ship again.

Only three runs were needed, up to the beginning of December. They followed the usual pattern, and must have gone without a hitch, for no incident of them remains in my memory.

I would have taken more note of them if I had known that they were to be the last. We had no premonition of the event, early in December, which was to bring *Mermaid*'s work to an end.

Yet I believe that at this time there had begun to lie upon all of us a sense that the war was leaving us behind, and that the pioneering days were passing. We found Lyness changed out of recognition. Where, in the first winter, we had lain alone at Baldry's buoy in a bay empty but for the *Greenwich* and the drifters, or had berthed at the little wooden pier, Ore Bay was now full of moored craft, and two new steel jetties had been completed and were festooned with shipping. Large notice boards proclaimed regular ferry schedules between the islands, and the big new seine-net boats, which had been requisitioned as ferries, left and arrived every few minutes.

Ashore, the old mud tracks were now wide metalled roads, thronged with motor traffic. The scatter of wooden huts had become streets of permanent brick buildings. The oil tanks were still there; they had been lined with brick against bomb splinters, but already they were becoming redundant, since some of the underground reservoirs were ready and tankers were discharging into them from the stone quay.

Through all this alien magnificence the *Mermaid* picked her way uneasily, not without pride at having helped to build it, but suspicious of the crowd and heavy with the sense that her era was passing.

At Scrabster, too, another chapter seemed to be ending with the onset of bad weather and the shortening days.

After *Harvester* had gone, Richard felt, perhaps rightly, that there was no longer enough for him to do. Bitterly as Margaret and I knew that we should miss him, we had to agree it was right that he should go.

If I have said little about Richard's part during the fourteen months he had been with "the firm", I think it is because he fitted so perfectly into the collective "we" and "us". The chief difference was that he did more than his share of the work and that he did it more equably.

Like John Carr, he made sure that I did not become too serious, and sometimes I used to suspect that he and Margaret had conspired to pull my leg. For instance, when the sentry box on the quay was blown down in a gale, Richard at once classified it as scrap and removed all the boards from the back of it for a little job he happened to have on hand. With mixed feelings, I watched the sentry stand the box up again, inspect it from every angle, walk through it and round it, and finally give himself up to mystified reflection; and my heart sank, as I realised that I should have to pass within feet of him every time I walked down the quay.

For Richard the curious game of Happy Families played by the selection boards turned out well.

He soon obtained a commission in the R.N.V.R., and joined the fleet of camouflaged fishing boats that served the French resistance forces via the coast of Brittany. He was second in command, under Lt. Daniel Lomenech, of the boat that brought out the family of "Remy" (Gilbert Renaud), the leader of the network called the Confrairie de Notre Dame. Later he was given his own command and had many adventures, including the loss of his propeller in a gale off Ushant, as the result of which he had to sail his boat home.

Of many successful operations, not the least was to smuggle past the German cordon of inspection an enormous potted azalea in full flower—a present from French soil for Madame Renaud in London.

18

HURRICANE

"...but I am not to say, it is a sea, for it is now the sky; betwixt the firmament and it you cannot thrust a bodkin's point."

A Winter's Tale

UNTIL THE night of the 7th–8th December 1941 we had not seriously wondered whether we should have wired our house down against the wind, as they did in Orkney.

Every winter there were three or four gales which could claw the roof off a wooden building by compounded forces of pressure and suction, if the angle were right. The fiend could even gain entry to a large gable end, by cracking the transverse beams and staving it in. The pressure upon an outside surface twenty feet by ten feet might be as much as a couple of tons. If that happened, the whole hut could be torn intact from its bed and lifted away to sea like a balloon. The sensible householder frapped the ridge of his roof with steel cables, well anchored in the ground on either side.

Our house at Scrabster, however, was just forty feet from the foot of the sheltering brae. It was five feet from the road; the road, with its two walls, accounted for thirty feet; and from the rear wall the ground began at once to rise.

The brae was a grass slope of about forty degrees, rising a hundred feet to the fields at the top, which still sloped upwards for half a mile or so, through another two hundred feet of vertical height, to the heather on the rounded crown of the ridge. The whole barrier curved from west through

north-west to north, forming, one would say, a perfect
shelter to the village and harbour from winds blowing
between those points. The worst gales were always westerly.
East gales might blow very hard for days at a time, but they
never had the power of those from the west. So we had not
been worried about our house—until the hurricane
arrived.

It announced itself by noise. Noise which had been
mounting, no doubt, for some hours, before it pierced to
our consciousness through sleep. For when we awoke fully
it had become the voice of a giant.

The onslaughts overrode the basic pervasive din, to
create sudden pockets of pressure, with a series of shaking
explosions exactly like the sound of heavy gunfire. It was
literally "blowing great guns". The vibrations quivered in
all the fabric of the house as the cataracts of air outside
hit it and roared round it.

The assaults were intermittent, for the gale was pouring
over the brae from the north-west, and on this (lee) side
its torrent was being broken by the barrier into whorls
and eddies. Momentarily there would be a complete calm;
and then another onfall would burst thundering upon our
thin walls until they shuddered under the attack.

This ebb and flow of fury acted strongly upon some
primitive part of us, to make the battle seem personal and
invest the attacker with a designing malignance, which
roused a senseless counter-rage.

To quieten our nerves, we rose in the greying dawn and
went out to make sure of *Mermaid*.

Outside, it was still possible to walk, though not to hold
a straight course. Progress with the wind astern was by a
series of rushes, braked desperately by wide-planted feet.
Visibility extended across the harbour, but not much
beyond, for the south quay was already receiving spray
from the hundred-yard drift of the harbour itself, and th

bay outside vanished into grey smother in a quarter of a mile, blanking out the Thurso and Claredon shores.

Huge swells, pressed in from seaward, lipped the quay's outside edge. Their roots tore the sand from the shelving floor and thickened them to an opaque and ghastly yellow. Here, they were faced square to the Thurso shore and so ran across the wind, which attacked them in flank, ripping their breaking tops away eastward in vast ladders of spray.

The shape of an anchored ship showed dimly on the limit of the visible circle. She was a cargo vessel, riding light, and seemed a fair size—a thousand tons or more. As each swell passed amidships, her keel showed simultaneously at bow and stern.

Mermaid was no longer safe at her berth on the west quay. Beneath the harbour surf there was a run from outside which threatened to snap her warps. Above the battering of the wind about our ears, we could hear the water hissing out of them and the thuds from the turns on cleats and samson post, as they snubbed the terrifying surges of the boat. We must shift her somehow into the corner, out of the worst of the swell.

The inmost end of the south wall was the most sheltered place; but there was not length enough ahead of *Benduff* for her to lie. Alongside *Benduff* the water was whipped into surf, but it was a harbour sea with a drift of only a hundred yards; and we thought the broadside pressure of the wind would help to hold her to *Benduff* against the more dangerous charging of the swell.

It took two hours of delicate, muscle-stretching work to shift her those twenty yards without damage. She could not be let go more than a few inches at a time, and then only upon warps which had been led, doubled, in three or four directions, and were eased or taken up in turn, with desperate watchfulness, round secure holds.

At last she lay safe, festooned with motor tyres, alongside *Benduff*. The wind screamed round her tall mast, and pressed her, grinding heavily, against her neighbour, but

the tyres took the rub and their friction checked her fore-
and-aft movement from the swell.

Skipper "Benduff" was in his wheelhouse, clad as usual
in cap and grey pullover, smoking placidly. His crew were
vainly trying to rescue a pile of naval stores, which the
swells were threatening to wash off the quay, and he was
viewing their efforts with chuckling unconcern.

" 'Morning, Skipper! What a day! Looks as if that lot'll
be gone by high water!' "

"They're no' mines, Mr Bridges—they're no' mines! No'
till they're aboord here! If they ask me, I shall say til them:
'Why did ye no' mak the quay higher? Why did ye no' pit
yeer stoores in a safe place!' " He chuckled richly. "Why
should I worry!"

All the same, he had sent the crew to do what they could.
And when he told us that he would keep an eye on the
Mermaid I felt greatly relieved.

We thought we might safely go to breakfast.

The heavy work had not yet stirred the bitter cold out
of our hands, but we were sweating emptily beneath our
clothes.

In the sudden stillness of the house we found we still
shouted at each other. Deliverance from streaming oilskins
and from jackets and ganseys, which had become stifling,
was a relief. There was a spark of content, too, in having
secured the ship and in the manning effect of exercise.
But we were too stunned and sickened by the wind to think
much of food. Though the house walls enclosed a patch of
calm air, in which our hands and faces burned, they also
acted as a detector, sorting out the separate sounds of the
wind, so that we seemed to be listening to its councils.

The thing was growing. As we sat and made pretence to
eat, the noise left us in no doubt of it. We moved about the
house, watching the shuddering frames, the thin back wall
behind the shelves breathing inwards, cursing ourselves
for not having wired the house down in good time, wondering if the weight of furniture and gear would hold it down

At about eleven o'clock we could stand the strain no longer. If the house went, it went: we could do nothing about it now. Nor could we do more about *Mermaid*. Skipper "Benduff" had six strong men who would do for her, if necessary, what for us was now beyond our power. This gale, in any case, was reaching a force in which that of human beings almost ceased to count. We decided we would get out into it, and, if the lighthouse path were traversable, fight along there and see if we could glimpse the state of affairs at Holburn Head. Even before breakfast, someone had shouted that green water was coming over the Head from the west.

We were rigging on our clothes again, when the door was hove open and crashed shut, as a streaming figure fell into the passage.

"Your boatie's hurt," he cried. "Ye'd better come doun!"

It was the assistant harbourmaster, another of the Sinclairs. It was a fighting day for him. His keen brown face streamed with spray, and his lip was lifting over his teeth.

"What's happened?"

"The steamer's come in—her that was in the bay. She's running wild, mon! We'll never hold her in this. The *Mermaid*'ll be lost if ye don't get her shifted!" He forced the door open, and was gone.

When we got outside for the second time, the world appeared to be in a state of dissolution. The screaming air was so full of water—whether rain or spray: spray I think most of it was—that solid objects only shivered through it like images in a worn film. It was difficult to stand or to focus—even to breathe. I was aware of short grass at my feet blasted into shifting furrows, like the fur on a rabbit's back. And then Margaret yelled into my ear, and I saw a few yards off the great bow of a ship, the hawse holes empty, and a forest of wires leading across the quay road to where a party of men, looking like drunken beetles, staggered about a trench. They were burying the salmon fishermen's

mooring anchors. They had prised out kerbstones from the
quay's edge to lay in front of the flukes. The anchors were
each seven feet long in the shank and weighed three hundredweight, and fortunately there were a dozen or more,
stored for the winter at the inner end of the quay.

The tide was almost at the turn. The wind had so banked
it up that the harbour was like a pot about to boil over,
and the bow of the steamer stood twenty feet above the
quay, its whole area exposed to the slantwise pressure. We
saw her name, *Sado*, and the painted Norwegian colours.
Then we saw a great hole in the quay, and remembered
that there had been a concrete bollard there.

Steering well clear of the trench diggers, we were being
blown past them, when a wire parted, with no audible
sound, but with a quick flash of fire.

Mermaid was where we had left her, alongside *Benduff*.
She still had her mast, but when we got near we could see
that the stem head and bulwarks were gone and that the
deck planking of the counter had been burst upwards. The
Sado's counter loomed very close over a great thrashing
screw, but its overhang threatened the mast rather than
the hull, and we could not understand what had happened.

In the shelter of his wheelhouse Skipper "Benduff"—in
oilskins now, his face streaming with water—explained
that, on first coming into harbour, the *Sado* had tried to
berth in her present position, but had torn out three
bollards and had fallen back broadside on to *Mermaid*
before his people were aware of what was happening. It
was obvious she might do the same again at any moment.
The first thing was to drag *Mermaid* astern.

The pressure was now such that Margaret and I could
have made no impression on the boat by ourselves. *Benduff*'s crew were very good. It took all six of them an hour
to shift her a hundred feet. Struggling from ship to ship
we handed the ends of warps and wrought desperately, as
the gale and the wash from *Sado*'s screw threatened to se

Mermaid's hull under *Benduff*'s counter and carry away the mast.

She was only just clear when *Benduff*'s turn came. The great counter fell back, the wind and the torque of the propeller dragging it to the right, so that it missed *Benduff*'s wheelhouse and settled over her stern, flattening the bulwarks and smashing boats and davits. We could hear the grind and crash even through the maniac roar of the storm.

But at last the tide was ebbing. Somehow they got hold of *Sado*'s head again, and with full power on her engines she slowly drew away from the wreckage she had made, and pushed inch by inch ahead until she was on the ground.

The *Mermaid* was a heartbreaking spectacle. Something —perhaps a propeller blade—had knocked off the top of her stempost. The ragged lump of wood, with gammon iron attached, had been prevented by the forestay from going over the side; it lay on deck, the slack forestay tangled with the starboard shrouds, whose rigging screws had been bent and cracked.

The rest of the damage had resulted from the squeeze. The bulwarks had gone all round; where they had not disappeared, both rail and stanchions had been broken in many places, leaving blackened stumps along the edge of the covering boards.

Luckily the main pressure had been abreast the cockpit, where the thrust was taken at deck level rather than at the waterline; yet, unluckily, there had been some projection on *Benduff*'s side at the point of bearing, which had caused heavy damage on the port side. There was a split six feet long in the deep mahogany plank of the coach roof and cockpit coaming. The cabin doors had been set an inch past each other and had jammed. Three of the topside planks were cracked, all at the same point. The deck planks of the port side-deck, abreast the cockpit, were cracked, and several of those abaft the cockpit had been broken and some had been burst upwards off the beams by the force of

the squeeze. A brief glance into the sail locker confirmed
that two of the beams there had been split.

These grievous hurts smote and agonised more than if
they had been in our own bodies. The *Mermaid* was more
than a home to us, more than a boat: she had been the very
core of our adventure. For a time we could only busy ourselves in setting up temporary rigging for the wobbling
mast, being more numbed now by the disaster than by the
gale, which, for the moment, had become something
altogether secondary and external: a phantom blast.

The credit side appeared more slowly. Surprise grew
upon us that the ship still floated. We levered the cabin
doors open, and found that the water was not even above
the cabin floor. Five minutes' pumping cleared it out. The
cabin roof was intact; neither beams nor carlines there
were damaged. And the propeller shaft turned easily.

It seemed a wonder of wonders that the engine started
at the first swing; but it and its mounting had been nowhere near the line of pressure. The frames were all hidden
by the boards of the ceiling, except for a few inches at the
top; the chances were that they were all right, except for
one or two in the critical area on the port side.

She would not sink; and she could still be moved under
her own power when the wind allowed.

Further than that our numbed brains would not go, in
the first desperate appraisal of this streaming, battered
thing, which had been our boat. She hove at her warps
beaten sideways by the rending force of the storm; her
planking blackened by spray and streaked with rope fibres
that looked, to our shattered imagination, like sweat
plastered hair.

The peak of the hurricane now became too enormou
to let the conscious reactive sense be occupied with any
thing but survival.

The landmarks of the world had so vanished that w
seemed already half out of the body, existing in a narrow
space, filled only with an insupportable imminence

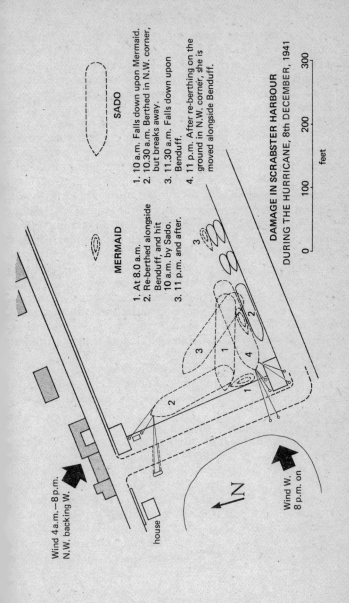

SADO

1. 10 a.m. Falls down upon Mermaid.
2. 10.30 a.m. Berthed in N.W. corner, but breaks away.
3. 11.30 a.m. Falls down upon Benduff.
4. 11 p.m. After re-berthing on the ground in N.W. corner, she is moved alongside Benduff.

MERMAID

1. At 8.0 a.m.
2. Re-berthed alongside Benduff, and hit 10 a.m. by Sado.
3. 11 p.m. and after.

DAMAGE IN SCRABSTER HARBOUR
DURING THE HURRICANE, 8th DECEMBER, 1941

0   100   200   300

feet

Wind 4 a.m.–8 p.m. N.W. backing W.

house

N

Wind W. 8 p.m. on

force, as in the moment of birth or death. The houses a
hundred yards away, even the shapes of the *Sado* and the
Benduff, were mere glooms behind vortices of spray.
Sounds were all fused and submerged into a single battering—an assault rather than a noise—through which speech
could travel only a distance of inches at the utmost pitch
of the lungs.

Only vertically overhead could the eye find a dizzy rest,
where the greyness was apparently still, like a pure jet of
steam or water, showing nothing but the faintest flicker to
betray its furious movement.

A forlorn wash of planks poked alongside through the
jetting surf, and we recognised the ruins of Geordie
Lindsay's boat—and felt a momentary thankfulness that
our own *Diadem* had been hauled out in front of our house.
Poor Geordie—he would get compensation, no doubt; but
his boat, bought years ago from a Norwegian ship, was
perfect for his job and had no doubt become an old friend.

We wondered if the house was still standing. *Sado*'s bulk
hid it. If it had gone someone would probably have told
us—and yet, with the *Sado* aground and safe for the time
being, and every man, who could be, under cover, it might
have collapsed unnoticed.

Mermaid was in a kind of equilibrium, which should not
be further threatened until *Sado* came off the ground again
towards midnight. We would have to keep watch all night
aboard.

We scrambled over the two seine-net boats inside us and
progressed, by hand as often as on foot, along the quay,
dropping flat whenever the wind flung us towards the
yellow crests that marched in majesty along its outside edge,
the troughs now so deep that the bottom weed showed in
the hollows as they passed. Dark funnels in the wrack above
them framed for an instant their white bursts high up the
sheltered bank beneath the Thurso road.

Once round the corner, on the inner quay, we saw that
the house still stood. Across the quay road was a huge

ragged slot, where two anchors had been dragged through
it when the *Sado* had fallen back on to the *Benduff*. Now, a
fresh web of wires led to new and more strongly fixed
points, against the time when the next flood tide would lift
her.

Apart from a burst window, our house was still un-
damaged. There was that much to be said for having a lot
of gear: it made good ballast! In a sick relief, we changed
our soaked clothes, drank hot coffee, and thereafter, for a
few hours, slept.

The wind had backed and reached its peak at about the
time we left *Mermaid*.

By midnight, when the *Sado* was again afloat, it had
eased to a point where her own crew, plus the crew of the
lifeboat, who had brought her in and tended her throughout the day, could contrive to shift her until she lay alongside *Benduff*. They shifted all the anchors, too, and
festooned her head with wire ropes leading to these and to
the yet-intact stone bollards at the corner. The wind was
now west, below hurricane force, but still blowing more
than a full gale. It blew directly on to the bows of the *Sado*
in her new position, and, coming now from inland, it had
cleared the air of spray, so that objects were seen in their
proper place again, and tatters of cloud were thinning,
high up, to show the stars.

The threat from the *Sado* was now to all craft moored
astern of her on the south quay. All vessels, including even
her fifteen-hundred-ton bulk, rocked to the tremendous
scend of the swell beating afresh into the harbour entrance
with the rising tide, and the wires from her bow snapped
in flashes of sparks with depressing regularity.

Like our neighbours, we had our engine running, ready
to cast off and back away if the loom of *Sado*'s counter
showed any signs of growing upon us. The dislimning dark
made it impossible to judge distance; and for hours we
either watched from *Mermaid*'s cockpit, dry at last, but

shivering in the freezing blast, or else scrabbled along the quay to watch for fireworks from the *Sado*'s snapping wires and confirm that enough still remained to hold her.

Gradually the pressure of the wind eased, and the tide fell, until, near morning, no more wires broke, engines were turned off, and the weary tension fell away. Our neighbours, the crew of the Wick boat *Fisher Boy*, asked us aboard for tea, and it was then that the picture, of which, in our troubles, we had seen only disjointed fragments, began to fill in.

The *Sado* was the villain of the piece, though she was scarcely to be blamed, for she had carried away both anchors and cables in the bay before signalling her S.O.S. The lifeboat had gone out to her, and its crew had thought they could bring her into harbour. Probably they did well to bring her in at all. Being unladen but only in ballast, a wind of that force made her practically unmanageable. She had knocked off a blade of her propeller on the pier head—we understood then why she could not keep clear of *Benduff* when she fell back the second time. In all, she had hit six vessels and done many thousands of pounds worth of damage.

At first, they had tried to beach her in the north-west corner, but her light draught forward and the high tide kept her bow clear of the sand until the tide fell. In the scend they could hold her head with wire alone. Curiously, she had not a single piece of rope aboard.

By morning, the wind had fallen away to a thin, bitter draught, that mourned about the washed spaces of the air.

The streaming world lay clear to sight again, spent, like ourselves, after the passing of the fury, and marvellously still, except for the loud, and now distinct, groaning of the surf.

The people of the village and of the ships stood here and there comparing notes, while the masters of the vessel which had been hurt made inventories of their damage and kept the *Sado*'s captain busy with their reports.

Word came from Orkney that over forty vessels had been blown ashore in the Flow.

We never heard whether the speed of that wind had been measured, or what distance its front had covered, or what ships it had sunk. At Scrabster, a three-hundred-foot ridge had stood in the path of its attack. The *Sado*, a ship of fifteen hundred tons, had snapped both cables within a quarter of a mile of the harbour mouth. The swells, into which she had been steaming at full power when her cables went, had been merely a run from the outside seas, bent at right angles to the wind into the shelter of the re-curving shore.

Some days later we paid our deferred visit to Holburn Head, and gazed in wonder at the acres up there that had been covered with grass and heather and were now a brown desert; where, upon a scarred bed of clay and rock, lay a litter of stones, some of them as big as tables: not dropped there, as one might imagine, by a receding ice-cap, but torn from the cliff face and flung upwards by solid water from the sea, a hundred feet below.

19

OTHER PEOPLE'S TROUBLES

"So these hosts are driven
By the relentless wind to rear and roar,
Topple and crash in thunderous discord
Against the smooth outpouring of the tide."

The Gate

THERE BLEW a gale on the 13th February from the north-east, which was not far short of the December hurricane.

A coaster lost her propeller in Wick Bay, went on to the rocks out of reach of the rocket line, and was battered to pieces with the loss of all hands.

Away to the north-east, Barnwell, with old Geordie McKay ("The President") and a boy, was coming south along the coast of Ronaldshay in his latest and rottenest acquisition, the *Nellie*, a sister ship of the *Shannon*. They were still running phosphate from the Westray wreck to Aberdeen.

The old Zulu was not fit for it. As she rolled in the beam seas, with sixty to seventy tons of dead weight in her hold, her seams began to open up. In that wind, on a lee shore, they could do nothing but pump and keep going. Before they reached the mouth of the Firth she was awash.

Perhaps, before she foundered, they had turned her towards the land; or perhaps she was forced in by wind and sea. Nobody knows. For nobody ever saw a plank of her again. The boy disappeared with her. But Barnwell and the President swam ashore; they actually got themselves, alive, through the break of a full gale on a rocky coast, and climbed fifty feet up the cliff, clear of the seas.

There they stuck, on a ledge, with sheer rock above and on both sides. And there, thirty-six hours later, those two old heroes were found, their bodies still warm. The *Nellie* had not been missed until reported overdue, and several miles of coast had then to be searched.

Barnwell was in his fifties, but the President was long past seventy, when they made that last play with the sea. The full gale had not beaten them, even without their ship; but only their own carelessness and the accidents of delay.

We thought a good deal about them both, going over in our minds the few pictures we had of them, and understanding now that we had never quite known what manner of men they were.

At Scrabster, the day before that gale, the glass fell seven-tenths between midday and dusk. It was a short, steel-eyed day, full of bleak menace. We did not need the rising gusts at dark to convince us that we were in for "one of the nights": one of the three or four worst nights of the winter, when the giants awoke and strode through the doorways of the world.

Mermaid was still in the Thurso River—it was the only time we ever felt devoutly thankful for that—and for once we went to bed without responsibility.

But sleep does not come easily in a great wind. The assault seems too personal and the threat too immediate to be ignored. And perhaps, tonight, the desperation of many men—two of whom I had known—came through the roaring air and muttered at the gates of the mind. The wind was still west of north-west, veering slowly, gaining in power, till we feared again for our shuddering house.

I lay awake, trying to picture what it would be like in the Firth, with a wind of perhaps a hundred miles an hour meeting the new-moon ebb, a river ten miles wide running at ten knots.

Seen from above, it would be a sea of white, a mass of hurrying drift like a cloud floor. But seen from a ship it would be chaos. I speculated vaguely on the height of the seas. What would they be—seventy, eighty feet? Probably not more than half that. The water was too shallow and the floor too broken. But they would not be what one imagined by the word "seas". They would be spouts, pits, precipices, great masses uprearing and falling, without order, anywhere, everywhere at once.

I thought of the cruiser that had lost her bridge there during the 1914–18 war. She might have been coming from the east on just such a night as this. As far as Duncansby she would have sheltered water, and that might have put her watchkeeper off his guard, perhaps, so that he came round the corner without reducing speed and met the first clean-cut tide-line of the sea walls before he realised what it was.

She would have staggered over the first. Then her bows would have dropped into the pit, and the last sight of those on her bridge would have been the foredeck driving into a glassy, white-lipped wall as into a mouth.

Presently, I left these morbid speculations, and dozed off to sleep.

Somewhere in the bad small hours I woke again, and became aware of a light, that glowed, far off, through the inferno beyond the window pane. After watching it for some time, I made certain that it was flickering: in fact, that it was a fire.

It lay in the direction of Thurso, but it was short of the town. It seemed to come from a point on the shore mid-way between Thurso and Scrabster, where there was a rocket house and a cottage built beside the ruins of an old Pictish broch.

The cottage must have gone on fire; perhaps there had been a blown spark from the hearth, or a spilt lamp. An old fisherman and his wife lived there. They would need all the help they could get on a night like this.

We turned out, intending to warn Myers and his fire party; but before we were into our clothes we heard the

ound of the brass bell that had been brought ashore from
he *Beech* to act as a fire warning; and when we went out
nto the screaming dark, cries and the flickering of torches
howed the party already starting off with the motor pump.

Myers told us to turn in again, promising to let us know
: we could help later on with shelter and food. So we went
nd lay down again, fully dressed, and dozed until the
indows began to turn from black to grey.

It was some time before we could see the ship.

The wind had gone into the north-east and was at its
eight, and the whole inner shore of the bay, from the
luffs under Scrabster House to the reefs and ledges
owards Thurso, was a white mass of bursting seas. For a
ong time the ship was indistinguishable in this smother,
or it was high water, and she had been holed on the reefs
nd was awash. We were watching for the cottage; and
resently we saw at that point the deck outline of a trawler,
ounded, bows to the shore, perhaps a hundred yards out
om the low cliff.

The seas were searching her whole length. Each burst at
er stern, burst again at her wheelhouse, gathered fresh
lidity along the winch deck, and exploded upwards in a
nal spout as it hit the six-foot break of the fo'c'sle.

The flames, then, had had nothing to do with the cottage,
ut had come from oil flares lit as distress signals by the
awler's crew. That must have been at low water; for no
re could be lit on board as she was at present.

As the light grew, the details of her upper works began
show between the white bursts, till at length her rigging
uld be seen, with men clinging high up in the shrouds.
nd—cheering sight—there came from the cliff the sudden
shing arc of a rocket.

We made a couple of gallons of strong coffee, into which
e emptied a bottle of rum, filled a big Thermos with
me of it and put the rest into two large kettles.

Then we rigged on layers of clothing, tied the kettles to
bicycle (when the wind blew into their spouts, it drove

the coffee out from under the lids!), and staggered up th
road towards the wreck.

There was now hail in the wind. It struck the face o
the cliff by the little rocket house and was swept upward
with the rising blast like a dust storm. The party workin
there round the tripod of the breeches buoy had a pre
carious lee; but wherever the hail struck, it cut so as to b
unfaceable.

The rocket party was down below on the rocks, havin
failed again and again from the cliff top, owing to the forc
and angle of the wind, to obtain a lodgment of the lin
upon any part of the ship where the crew could reach i
They were doing no better now. As we arrived, we hear
the rush and saw the flash of the rocket, soaring over th
ship—a true shot, fair between the masts; but the win
blowing slightly from one side, once more caught the bigl
of the line and swept it clear.

The bow of the trawler was no more than seventy yarc
away. From the cliff top, which was here only forty to fif
feet above the sea, every detail of her deck could be see
The seas swept and burst over it continuously, so that tl
rigging was the only part left of her where men could liv
They had been clinging there for hours—eight of them
in that fury of wind and hail and spray, some without o
skins, some even without seaboots, which had been fill
and dragged off their legs by the seas.

The rocket party had shifted their ground, and fir
again, and at last the bight of the line caught the mast ju
above the heads of the men in the shrouds.

We wondered if they would have strength to haul o
and lash the block. One man, who turned out to be t
skipper, got the job done. It was agony to watch him wor
drawing on everything he had to save his own life and t
lives of his crew. When he had finished, the roar of che
ing must have reached him, even above the gale.

The shore party, under Mr Miller and Alec Sincla
now worked like demons upon the hawser. They had mo

elp than they needed, so, having got a fire going in the rocket house, we crouched in the lee of a bank, more or less clear of the lashing onslaughts of the hail, and watched them.

Soon the breeches buoy was shuttling to and fro, and the crew were being helped into the rocket house.

The worst sufferers were the young fellows and the engineers. They were dazed from shock and cold, their faces were drained of colour, and they could not hold a mug to their lips.

The mate, on the other hand, was cheerful and conversational. He told us that this made the fourth time he had been wrecked and he supposed it wouldn't be the last! Not to be outdone in courtesy, after drinking our coffee, he pulled a small, soaked bar of chocolate out of the pocket of his blouse and presented it to Margaret.

The only man completely unmoved was the skipper. He was a solid, well-built man of perhaps fifty, with a magnificent face, heavily lined, with a square jaw and deep-sunk eyes. The rather thick lips, yellowish skin, and black hair hinted at a mixture of blood in which there may have been negro strain. He behaved as though he had just been rowed ashore for a drink at the inn. For eight hours he had been clinging in soaked clothes to a ship's rigging in a winter gale at a temperature near freezing. Yet his hand did not tremble; and, though he spoke little, his voice was normal. Probably he was already thinking about how to salvage his ship, for he was owner as well as skipper.

He was an extraordinary chap, typical, probably, of the carelessness, as well as the incredible toughness and persistence, of trawlermen.

He had arrived, outward bound, the previous afternoon, and had anchored in the bay. But in spite of the warning he must have had from his barometer, he neglected either to come into the harbour before the gale, or to keep enough steam to prevent dragging after it had begun.

He had dragged both anchors, and had evidently had steam enough to lift them, for they were both in the hawse pipes when the ship went aground. With engines dead, her bows had been blown off and she had gone in bows first right beneath the rocket house. As the tide rose, she drove further and further in, and it was during this time, when the seas had begun to sweep her decks, that three of her crew had been washed overboard and drowned before they could reach the rigging.

At three in the afternoon, when the tide had ebbed and the gale had died out into a gentle breeze, their bodies lay in the cold sunshine upon the beach, flung there in the casual, unmistakable attitudes of things used and done with.

The finances of such a disaster were beyond our understanding. We heard a rumour that the ship was not insured, and yet by this time she must have been, if only under the compulsory business scheme of the Government.

At all events, the *Metinda*, whose services cost £50 a day, came and worked upon her for a month. She was patched, refloated, and towed to Aberdeen, where no doubt her engines would have had to be stripped completely and put together again before she could once more be ready for sea. And she was a small North Sea trawler of an old type!

We went back that afternoon to a belated meal, thinking soberly of the luck of the game, and that, so far, we had been treated very gently.

At Scrabster, the *St Ola* was in. There had been no one to take her lines. Every man had been out watching or helping with the wreck. Captain Swanson had laid her alongside at the height of the gale and berthed her with his own crew!

20

WIND-UP

"Partir, c'est toujours mourir un peu."

FOR MARGARET and me there was a misery about winding-up that I would keep out of this story if I could. The ending of any adventure in which life has been lived fully and intensely is a sorry business. Yet there must be an end as there has been a beginning. It is just one of those things.

After the hurricane we had beached the *Mermaid* at the top of the December springs in a quiet corner of the Thurso River. She would not have been safe in Scrabster, unattended, and we felt we had to get away. Weather had never seriously upset us, up to this, but the weather for the past four months had been terrible, and no doubt the effect of working at full pressure through three sub-arctic winters had become cumulative. After seeing the ship safe and taking the first dips in the sea of paper work—insurance claims, notifications, and so on—resulting from the smash, we went south for a month to try and forget about it.

When we returned, we had to face the fact that our job was done. *Mermaid* had filled a gap caused in the early days of the war through sheer insufficiency and disorganisation. A seine-net boat or a drifter would have done her work far more safely and easily; and now such craft were once more available. She could not be used again without major repairs. For these she would have to go to Buckie, and it might be midsummer before they could be finished. Even then it was doubtful whether more work in her old line could be found for her.

Briarbank was running steadily and carrying out her specialised work of ferrying heavy gear between the islands. But would we be justified in sitting at Scrabster merely to write letters about a ship we owned but never saw, nowadays, more than once a month? As for the *Diadem*, she could never be more than a make-weight to help us exist. And we were still hopeful enough to believe that we ourselves could be used for something more to the purpose than lobster fishing during the rest of the time that the war might last.

The first job was to bring the *Mermaid* back to the harbour for temporary repairs, since nothing could be done to her whilst she lay in the river.

We found her in a sorry state. The local youth of Thurso —that particular age-group so aptly called in Scotland "the loons"—had smashed the skylight and several of the cabin portholes, and her cabin was a soaked mess. She seemed even further up the bank than when we had left her; perhaps succeeding tides had been raised above their normal height by wind.

It took four spring tides to float her off. During the first two spells we tried unsuccessfully to lever her bow clear by means of wooden baulks. We dared not rock her over on to her outside bilge, in case her keel should still stick until the water left her; she would then have canted outwards, and come to rest horizontally on the outward slope of the bank, so that the next tide would have filled her.

There was no choice left but to remove her ballast or to dig away the bank beneath her keel. We thought the latter process would be safer, with the mast in her, and also slightly less prolonged; and so, for several days before the top of the next spring tides, we trailed on foot the two-mile road to the river, pushing a bicycle lashed with picks and bars and shovels. The ground along her keel was of flat stones mixed with mud, and she had not sunk far into it. But the first grave we dug was not deep enough. We had to enlarge it into a shelf eighteen inches deep during the following fortnight, before at last we could lever her over the edge and set her free.

There was not much we could do at Scrabster beyond making her barely fit for the journey to Buckie. We had to wait for a really settled spell of weather, and it was the middle of May before we set out.

Perhaps I was hopelessly sentimental; yet I could see again the expression on old Mr Sandison's face when we took *Harvester* out of St Monance, and I knew that he would have understood what we felt and what we remembered, as the *Mermaid* swung out past the pierheads on her last—her fifty-eighth—passage of the Firth.

At Buckie we had several days of errands and work until it was certain that the ship's gear was safely stowed and arrangements solidly made for herself to be hauled out and repaired.

On the first day, a pair of urchins watched us from the edge of the quay with interest and alarm.

"Hist, mon," said one. "Coom awa'! They're Norrvegians, I tell thee!"

"Na," replied his companion, disdainfully, "they're nobbut a man and his wifie!"

In the Marine Hotel, to which we adjourned after our cooking gear had gone into store, we met a charming young man in the uniform of the Norwegian army, whose name was Nordahl Grieg. We did not know then that in the past two years he had become Norway's national poet. His loss, six months later, with the crew of a bomber over Berlin, must have been as poignant for the Norway of his time as that of Rupert Brooke had been for Englishmen of the previous generation.

At Scrabster, the sorry business of disposing of our assets went on slowly through the summer.

We had no difficulty in selling *Diadem* and the lobster gear.

Parting with *Briarbank* was a very different matter.

It soon appeared that the ordinary rights of ownership

in a vessel even of her size no longer existed. No vessel could now be transferred without permission from the Ministry of War Transport, and this permission could be indefinitely withheld or indefinitely delayed, quite regardless of any consequences to the owner, whose business was merely to look after and pay for every detail of his ship's maintenance whilst the authorities made up their minds.

Throughout the summer the paper battle went on assuming the same nightmare quality as the *Harvester* business, eighteen months before. I had undertaken another piece of work in the south, to start on the 1st November—far enough ahead, I thought, to give ample time for disposing of *Briarbank* and winding up our remaining affairs. Margaret went on ahead of me. But by the end of September permission to transfer the ship was as far away as ever, despite numerous offers to buy. A gentleman from Sheffield was apparently pulling strings to have the ship requisitioned and handed over to his firm, so that he might then hire her to the Government for laying seaplane moorings. He was not interested in buying her. For a moment I almost wished that I had had both the nerve and the contacts to work out something like this myself, and reflected on the truth of the old saying that one half of the world doesn't know how the other half live. A week later, the agents in London wrote to say that they had heard unofficially that the requisition was to go through.

I felt I could not stand any more of this. If that was the way it was to be played, I thought, then that was the way I would have to play it. I sat down and put the whole case to a friend who could beat a much bigger drum than the gentleman from Sheffield, and asked him whether, if he thought my case sound, he could help me out.

Within four days, thanks entirely to his personal intervention, I was in direct touch with the Parliamentary Secretary to the Minister of War Transport, and forty-eight hours later permission for transfer to the last of the many intending purchasers had been placed in the agents' hands.

I was glad that Margaret had gone south ahead of me and so was spared the final good-byes.

Too final—so many of them. Kirk, John Carr, Captain Swanson, Captain Shearer, rough Jim Barnwell, tough old Geordie McKay—to you, and to many others who have not yet gone on so long a journey, I shall never speak again. We worked hard together in those three years; and for that reason—and perhaps because the war did not deal too extremely with me—I shall never be able to think of your going with indifference or shrug my shoulders at your memory. It was more than a little insignificant job of work that we did, in a place few people have ever heard of. In those years we put all we had into an end outside ourselves, and for all else we did not give a damn.

It is a pity that it should have taken a war to make the opportunity for this—war, which leaves nothing but ash heaps. Now that war has been reduced to a rearrangement of atoms, an electronic calculation, outside humanity, it seems we must try to find the peaks of life in what passes for peace. That is going to be much more difficult; for, having bodies, we cannot find content unless we use them, and, having bound our existence to the confines of a factory, we must do no less than rediscover the world.

There are too many of us in this little island. We spend half our time trying not to tread on one another's feet. And we try, equally desperately, to express ourselves, to be people, not just "the holder of this card". Utopia is not Subtopia. Freedom must be physical, as well as mental and spiritual, and it is axiomatic that freedom of any kind decreases with density. The "concentration" camp is the final example. Ten hours away there is Canada, into one of whose lakes England could be dropped, and it has a population only twice that of one of England's towns. I do not think that youth is going to be satisfied much longer with four walls and flights of theory; nor with the carefully edited pornography that the theorists are content to see handed out to it as a substitute for air and space. Youth is both keen and generous, and it is getting bored stiff.

Intellectual adventure by itself is not enough. Sanity is largely a matter of humility, and nobody can be either humble or sane who imagines that by an exertion of intellect alone he can find all the answers. Intellect is an essential tool, but the situation so constantly outruns its best endeavours that, without trust—in what, exactly, it does not seem to matter, so that it be both beneficent and external—there would soon be madness or collapse.

In shelter, one may never learn this. In the furnaces of human hate and misery, one may be scorched in the process. Great natural forces are the surest and kindest teachers. A gale at sea presents a majesty and a beauty that require no formula or liturgy to make them real, and impresses very quickly upon anyone who is out in it the limits of his own strength and of his own intelligence. To be forcibly made aware of these limits is the true shrift; for then there is nothing left, and the blank can only be filled by trust—which is also love and reverence—if a man is to remain master of himself and be at peace.

The strong tides ebb and flow. If they have given me any certainty it is this: that I have known no heaven lovelier than this natural world, and that to have been next to it, even for a moment, is to have worshipped and to have been alive.

As Alfie drove me in the rackety old Pentland bus for the last time up the long slope out of the village, and I watched the great beak of Hoy opening clear of the Head and remembered that Margaret had never seen it from below, a plan came into my mind for returning some day to Scrabster. I hoped that we might be able to come back and look at the islands from a very different point of view: the view from a little cutter, free to sail where she would. Unvisited yet were the fjords of Stronsay and Sanday, the great sea-lochs to the west—Tongue and Eriboll—and a place with a name of wonder, the Red Heads of Eday. No cargo and no Gates, no scheduled route, no vigilant patrols. And—best of all—no bureaucrats! It would not be the same—never quite the same again. But I longed to go back.

That cruise is still a dream.

In the autumn of 1945, still working against time, Margaret and I brought the *Mermaid* south—an anxious journey, amongst minefields and wreckage, against the head winds of the equinox—and said good-bye to her at Shoreham. Good-bye! Sometimes I have thought I should die of that word.

From a recent Lloyds list I see that our ship is still afloat and has moved to Wales, to waters where she once passed, not so far from the place where her cargo was made.

EPILOGUE

(THE BOAT TO HER CREW)

If, in your world of blood and fire,
　　Through which you ever strive to ply
Your boat of life amid the dire
　　Storms of the all-encircling "I"—

If you, in face of sky and steel,
　　Jets, atoms, test-tubes, and the vote,
Can some capacity to feel
　　Grant to a little, battered boat;

Then, in your course from goal to goal,
　　Will this small voyager of the sea
—Since you've endowed it with a soul—
　　Sail with you through eternity.

Wood, rope, and flesh into the fog
　　Of death and decay the tides dismiss,
Yet life was written in the log—
　　Not life itself can alter this:

This, when the glass is falling fast
　　And skies are stripped for dirty weather,
This, from the proud, clean-winded past,
　　That somewhere, once, we sailed together!

On the following pages are details of Arrow books that will be of interest.

WINGED ESCORT

Douglas Reeman

As the grim years of the Second World War go by, the destruction of Allied shipping mounts. Out of the terrible loss of men and ships, the escort carrier is born.

At twenty-six, fighter pilot Tim Rowan, RNVR, is already a veteran of many campaigns. Now he joins the escort carrier *Growler* – a posting which takes him first to the bitter waters of the Arctic and all the miseries of convoy duty to Murmansk, and then south to the Indian Ocean and the strange new terror of the Japanese Kamikaze. . . .

COVENANT WITH DEATH
John Harris

'Your generation was born to suffer in this war, but it's got to be won by whoever falls, and we rely on you. Never mind your pals. Just keep going.'

Fine words – and for a few hours the men believed them.

Next day they were dead, torn to pieces by the machine guns in the first few minutes of the Battle of the Somme.

This is the story of those men. The story of their courage, their trust and their final betrayal.

THE MERCENARIES
John Harris

Yesterday's heroes . . . today's mercenaries

For World War I air-ace Ira Penaluna, peace brings frustration and disillusionment. Desperate to continue flying, he accepts an offer to go to China as commander of the ramshackle airforce of General Tsu, a local war lord.

With him he takes a bizarre trio of flying misfits:

PAT – the boozy, bragging Irishman, more interested in bar-hopping than flying.

SAMMY – the mechanical genius with a weakness for oriental beauties.

ELLIE – former woman stunt-pilot, tough and skilled in the air, tender and vulnerable in bed.

But before long, what began as a joyride becomes a desperate flight for life. For after centuries of poverty and exploitation, China is rising against brutal, corrupt rulers like General Tsu. And Penaluna's band of adventurers are branded mercenaries

THE MUSTERING OF THE HAWKS
John Harris

1917. The average life expectancy of a flier on the Western Front is three weeks. Inexperienced young men of the Royal Flying Corps are hurled into vicious dogfights over the trenches, often in inferior machines without adequate training, to be slaughtered by the German aces.

Into this hell comes Ira Penaluna, nineteen years old and in love with flying.

As the men who have become his friends die one by one, Penaluna realizes that in a world where skill, speed and killer-instinct are all, there is only one way to survive – learn to think like a hawk.

DANGER HAS NO FACE

James Hutchison

June 1944. A man dropped from a lone Stirling bomber into enemy-occupied France. A man with a new name, a new identity – and a new face.

Months previously, he had been known to the Gestapo as an important SOE operative working from London. Now, after extensive plastic surgery, he was Colonel Hastings, assigned to what was called 'a hazardous uniformed operation behind the enemy lines'.

Here for the first time James Hutchison – alias Colonel Hastings, later known as 'the Scarlet Pimpernel of the Maquis' – tells his own amazing story.

'Stranger than fiction . . . a truly extraordinary tale' Alasdair Maclean, *Scots Magazine*

DESTROYER

Ewart Brookes

'The best book on the subject I have ever read' Douglas Reeman

'Seek out and attack the enemy'

The motto of those who serve in destroyers sums up the magnificent history of this fighting ship.

Destroyer is the story of a breed of ship that has inspired more loyalty among the men who sailed and fought in them, provided more stories of gallantry, high adventure and hard-fought action than any other in recent naval history.

'A thrilling account of the role of a brave breed of fighting ship in two World Wars' *Evening News*

DEATH OF A DIVISION

Charles Whiting

They called it the ghost frontier . . .

December 1944. With the Germans in retreat, the 106th Allied Division were moved up to the frontier between Germany and Belgium. The war was apparently over on this frontier and they were the greenest division ever to be sent into the front line.

Within days, the 106th found themselves in the path of Von Manteuffel's mighty Panzer 5th Army – a quarter of a million men set on a last desperate offensive.

The 'Golden Lions' were trapped in one of the most disastrous miscalculations of the war – and the battle that followed was a frenzy of bloody chaos.

HOW WE LIVED THEN

A history of everyday life during the Second World War

Norman Longmate

Norman Longmate gives the reader a fascinating chronicle of the war years covering every corner of civilian life from the horrors of the blitz to the miseries of dried eggs and the five-inch bath.

'A book which has had me chuckling and sighing and tut-tutting and remembering as rarely before' *Daily Mail*

'From stirrup pumps to spam, Mr Longmate's marvellous comprehensive panorama of the six shattering years misses nothing' *Sunday Telegraph*

'Quite the best social chronicle of the period I have read. It really does give the authentic feel of what life in Britain was like for ordinary people' *Spectator*

Bestselling war books from Arrow

All the books listed below are available from your bookshop or newsagent or you can order them direct. Just tick the titles you require and complete the form below.

☐	DESTROYER	Ewart Brookes	75p
☐	THE MERCENARIES	John Harris	75p
☐	THE MUSTERING OF THE HAWKS	John Harris	70p
☐	ARMY OF SHADOWS	John Harris	90p
☐	THE FOX FROM HIS LAIR	John Harris	90p
☐	BLOOD BRIGADE	Don Houghton	65p
☐	COLUMN OF THIEVES	Don Houghton	90p
☐	DANGER HAS NO FACE	James Hutchison	90p
☐	WAR IN A STRINGBAG	Charles Lamb	£1.25
☐	STRIKE FROM THE SEA	Douglas Reeman	90p
☐	THE PRIDE AND THE ANGUISH	Douglas Reeman	90p
☐	SEND A GUNBOAT	Douglas Reeman	85p
☐	THE DESTROYERS	Douglas Reeman	90p
☐	RENDEZVOUS — SOUTH ATLANTIC	Douglas Reeman	95p

Postage _____

Total _____

ARROW BOOKS, BOOKSERVICE BY POST, PO BOX 29, DOUGLAS, ISLE OF MAN, BRITISH ISLES

Please enclose a cheque or postal order made out to Arrow Books Limited for the amount due including 8p per book for postage and packing for orders within the UK and 10p for overseas orders.

Please print clearly

NAME ....

ADDRESS ....

....

Whilst every effort is made to keep prices down and to keep popular books in print, Arrow Books cannot guarantee that prices will be the same as those advertised here or that the books will be available.